The Edge of the Sea of Cortez

Tidewalkers' Guide to the Upper Gulf of California

Betty Hupp & Marilyn Malone
Drawings by Marilyn Malone

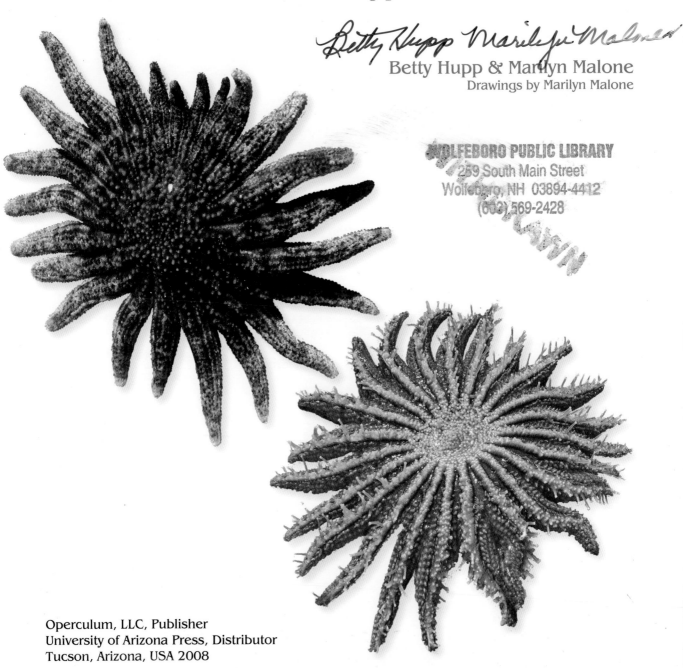

Operculum, LLC, Publisher
University of Arizona Press, Distributor
Tucson, Arizona, USA 2008

This book is affectionately dedicated to our families
who share our love for the edge of the sea.
Betty Hupp and Marilyn Malone

Foreword and Seaward

It is a rare beach walker on the edge of the Sea of Cortez who has not been captivated and mystified by the strange creatures slipping under rocks or burrowing into the sand and mud underfoot. As you leaf through this book you will find that you have discovered a treasure. It represents a dream come true for its authors, Betty Hupp and Marilyn Malone. Thirty-five years ago, when they and their families first discovered the tide pools of Puerto Peñasco, Mexico, few references were available that contained information about the sea life teeming between the twice-daily tides. At that time they dreamed of writing a book to fill the void. Recent explorations with University of Arizona marine biologists and research experts at CEDO* inspired the authors to create this user-friendly beach guide to help unravel its mysteries.

Incredibly diverse life forms and habitats are easily accessible to visitors at this interface between desert and sea. With sensitivity and accuracy, the authors have designed a tapestry that interweaves the life stories of seashore animals and their intertidal homes. Because the creatures are extremely vulnerable to human actions, we must respect their environment and take care to put them back into the special nooks or crannies where they are found. CEDO is proud to support this work of art and science as a resource for the curious naturalist in each of us. The alluring photographs and hands-on style make it a lively and entertaining book that sets a new standard for seashore field guides everywhere.

Peggy Turk Boyer
Executive Director, CEDO
*Intercultural Center for the Study of Deserts & Oceans

To order copies of this book contact:
www.uapress.arizona.edu, Distributor
Telephone 800-426-3797

or *www.cedointercultural.org*
PO Box 44208, Tucson, AZ 85733
Telephone 520-320-5473

or Operculum, LLC, Publisher
PO Box 85834, Tucson, AZ 85754
Telephone 520-296-7494

The Edge of the Sea of Cortez

The Sea of Cortez, also known as the Gulf of California, is framed by the Mexican mainland states of Sonora and Sinaloa and the peninsula states of Northern and Southern Baja California. Once called the Vermillion Sea, its long, narrow shape results in tidal extremes that provide a unique home for a rich diversity of marine life. Its beautiful water sustains those who live along its shores, entices tourists from all over the world, and beckons marine scientists to discover its secrets.

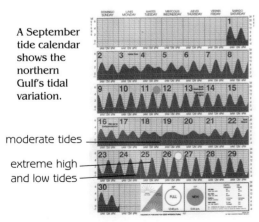

A September tide calendar shows the northern Gulf's tidal variation.

moderate tides

extreme high and low tides

Where to Find Specimens

You will experience a moveable visual feast as you search for seashore creatures throughout the intertidal zones. You are likely to encounter an increasing variety of animals when you follow an outgoing tide as the water recedes. The most likely places to find interesting specimens are:

On rock surfaces

chiton   snail laying eggs   limpet

On, under, beside or between rocks

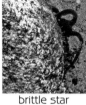

sponge   barnacles   limpet   chiton eggs   brittle star

In tidepools

brown algae   fireworm   hydroid   red algae   nudibranch

Look in a child's beach pail or plastic aquarium. Children are very good at finding and catching critters to examine.

brittle star   shrimps   fish

In reef holes or crevices

spiny urchin   pencil urchin   lumpy claw crab

Under reef ledges or bridges

yellow sponge   anemone   sun star

two pistol shrimps

crab

flatworm

brittle star

flatworms   limpet

A clear plate and an inverted bucket make an impromptu studio for viewing and photographing reef specimens.

Overhanging coquina ledge

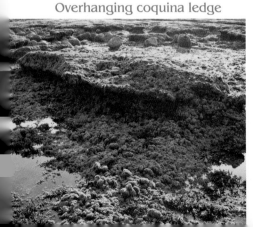

Overhanging coquina ledges and reef bridges are found in extreme low tidal habitats. These provide safe havens for animals that cannot endure the pounding of brutal waves, but can tolerate air exposure for brief periods while the tide is out.

Reef bridge

2

Zonation and Intertidal Habitats

This book describes the sea life between the farthest reaches of high and low tides on rocky, sandy and muddy shores. The lowest tidal habitat of the living reef is rarely available or even visible to tidewalkers.

Intertidal zones are more easily distinguishable when viewed from afar than up close on the beach. Shoreline environments at the top of the tidal zones range from sea cliffs and steep rocky shores to broad stretches of dry dunes above the damp sand in the splash zone.

The strandline or high tide line shows how far up the most recent high tide reached along shore. Bits of algae with egg capsules or air bladders, fish or bird bones, feathers, driftwood or other flotsam litter the sand along the strandline after each high tide. Isopods, sand fleas and other minute creatures live high and dry along the strandline.

Intertidal Zones:

The extreme low intertidal zone is exposed to air only a few hours each month. The animals are almost always under water.

The mid intertidal zone is covered and exposed by most tides daily, and the animals must survive in air or water.

The high intertidal zone is exposed to air and covered by sea water alternately with each tide.

The splash zone is mostly dry sand, seldom moistened by sea water.

Pelagic Habitat
In the pelagic habitat creatures live only in the water entirely off shore beyond the lowest tides.

Littoral Habitat
In the littoral habitat creatures live in intertidal zones between the highest and lowest tides, in water or air, on or under rocks and reefs, and in tide pools.

Benthic Habitat
In the benthic habitat creatures live in sand and mud sediments on the sea bed, or in moist sand or mud at the high tide line.

Phyla of Common Shoreline Invertebrates

Porifera
sponges

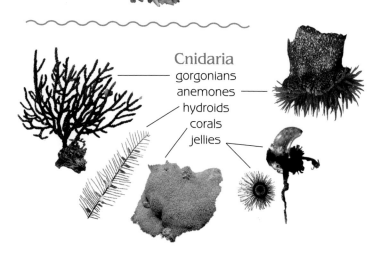

A phylum is one of the broad divisions in the plant or animal kingdoms. Phyla of the animals and plants discussed here are those most commonly encountered in the northern Gulf of California.

Phylum Porifera
Phylum Cnidaria
Phylum Platyhelminthes
Phylum Nemertea
Phylum Annelida
Phylum Sipuncula
Phylym Echiura
Phylum Mollusca
Phylum Arthropoda
Phylum Ectoprocta
Phylum Echinodermata
Phylum Chordata
Phylum Anthrophyta
Phylum Chlorophyta
Phylum Rhodophyta
Phylum Phaeophyta

Cnidaria
gorgonians
anemones
hydroids
corals
jellies

Annelida
segmented worms
sand worms
fireworms
featherdusters
tube worms

Platyhelminthes
flatworms

Nemertea
ribbon worms

Sipuncula
peanut worms

Echiura
spoon worms

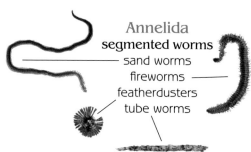
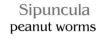

Mollusca
cephalopoda
octopuses
gastropoda
limpets
snails
sea hares
sea slugs
nudibranchs
polyplacophora
chitons

Mollusca
bivalves
clams
mussels
oysters
pen shells
scallops

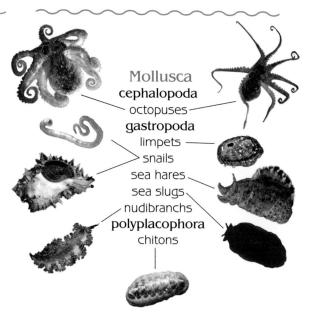

Phyla of Invertebrates (continued), Vertebrates, Algae and Plants

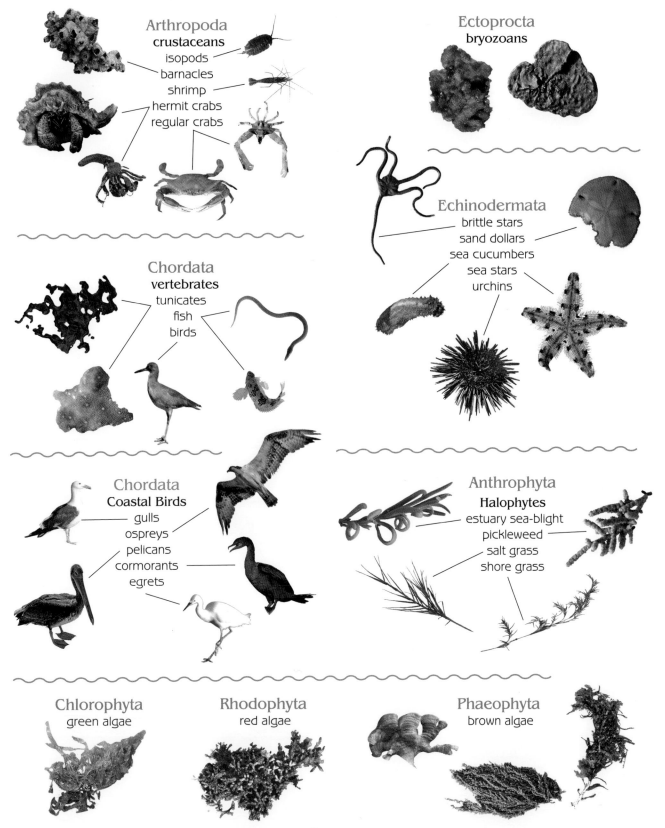

Arthropoda
crustaceans
isopods
barnacles
shrimp
hermit crabs
regular crabs

Ectoprocta
bryozoans

Echinodermata
brittle stars
sand dollars
sea cucumbers
sea stars
urchins

Chordata
vertebrates
tunicates
fish
birds

Chordata
Coastal Birds
gulls
ospreys
pelicans
cormorants
egrets

Anthrophyta
Halophytes
estuary sea-blight
pickleweed
salt grass
shore grass

Chlorophyta
green algae

Rhodophyta
red algae

Phaeophyta
brown algae

At the Rocky Shore

Rocky Shores: Reefs, Rocks and Tide Pools

Coquina reef "shell hash" contains familiar shell shapes.

Animals and plants cling to, hide under and live on and between the surfaces of rocky shores. This diversity of micro habitats yields a rich variety of living creatures, each adapted to its niche.

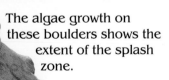

coquina

coquina surface

Basalt, granite and coquina provide different habitats. Geological processes have compressed shells, sand and organic material into coquina reefs that are softer and more porous than the basalt and granite rocks that also characterize rocky shores.

basalt boulders

basalt surface

granite boulders

granite surface

The algae growth on these boulders shows the extent of the splash zone.

algae growth

Seaweeds

Seaweeds are called the plants of the sea. Unlike earth plants, they get nutrients through their blades. Tidepool residents hide among algae clumps, nibble on algae blades and stay wet under algae when the tide is out. Each species has its own growing season.

Green and brown algae flourish on this reef.

Green Algae
~~~ Chlorophyta

Most intertidal algae need a place to anchor, so the rocky shoreline abounds with a variety of seaweeds attached to the reef, rocks and shells. The textures include soft, fuzzy, dense, tangled, hard, slippery and rough.

Dead Man's Fingers
Codium sp.
Alga Verde
clumps to 12" wide

If you touch the dead man's fingers algae, you will know why it has its common name.

blade

Sea Lettuce
Ulva rigida
Alga Verde
single blades to dense patches of varying sizes

The holdfast looks like a root, but it is not. It holds the algae to reefs and rocks with a glue-like secretion but does not provide a conduit for nutrients.

holdfast

Green Turf Seaweed
Valoniopsis pachynema
Alga Verde
clumps to 12" wide

Red Algae ~~~ Rhodophyta

Some red algae look like plants; others resemble coral because they are heavily calcified.

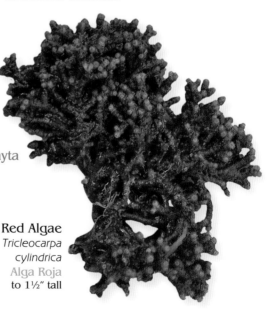

Red Algae
Tricleocarpa cylindrica
Alga Roja
to 1½" tall

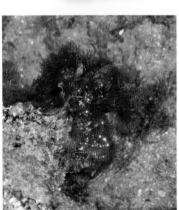

Red Algae
Gelidium sp.
Alga Roja
clumps to 12" wide

Brown Algae 〜 Phaeophyta

Seaweeds grow among the rocks in clumps, mats or strands and belong to three groups: green, red and brown, based on the predominant photosynthetic pigment. Colors can be misleading, however, so they are not reliable for positive identification.

Sargassum mats

Sargassum drapes

Sargassum
Sargassum sinicola
Sargasso
Strands of varying sizes may cover entire reefs.

bladder pods

blades

Several rocky shore Sargassum species, also called bladder wrack, have round pods or bladders full of air. The pods keep the blades on top of the water, providing maximum exposure to sunlight. At low tide Sargassum lies on the reef and drapes over ledges, keeping the surface moist. It shelters many tidepool residents.

Bubble gum algae looks like its namesake, but it's crunchy and slippery underfoot, not sticky.

Bubble Gum Algae
Colpomenia tuberculata
Alga Café
thallus (body) to 6" diameter

Bubble Gum Algae
Colpomenia sinuosa
Alga Café
thallus to 6" diameter

padina cluster

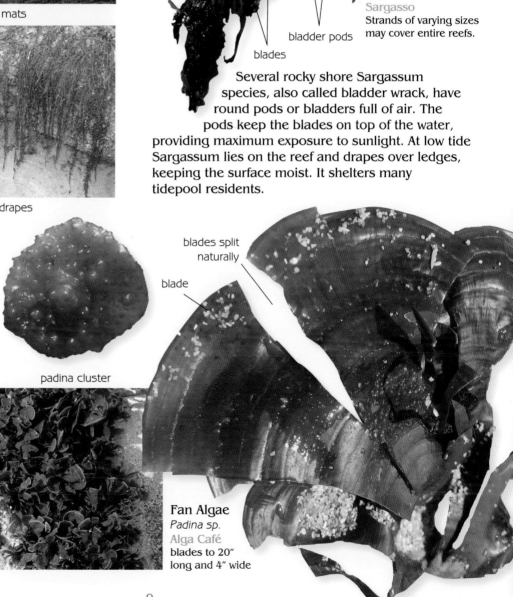

blades split naturally

blade

Fan Algae
Padina sp.
Alga Café
blades to 20" long and 4" wide

9

Sponges ～～～ Porifera

Sponges spread their colorful shapes over the rocky reef, filtering sea water through their bodies to extract microscopic tidbits from the currents. They are among the world's simplest organisms, having no brain, muscles or nerves.

may irritate the skin!

Calcareous Sponge
Leucetta sp.
Esponja
clumps to 6" wide

Volcano Sponge
Panamic Red Sponge
Fire Sponge
Tedania nigrescens
Esponja de Fuego
spreads up to 2' across

These sponges exhibit two growth patterns: compact and spreading.

sponge hole

Boring Sponge
Cliona sp.
Esponja
patchy areas on surfaces

Yellow patches are boring sponge.

Boring sponges use chemicals to make homes (and holes) in shells and rocks.

Brown Carpet Sponge
Terpios zeteki
Esponja
to several feet across, ½" thick

Sponge
Halichondria sp.
Esponja
spreads to 1'

oscula

Small animals hide in sponge water passages.

oscula

Sponges belong to bony, glass or spongy groups, depending on the type of internal structure. A loupe is useful to see the details.

water flow

osculum

spicules form structure

pores let water in

flagellate cells gather food

White sponges grow around urchin spines.

sponge water exchange system

Colonial Anemones ～～ Cnidaria

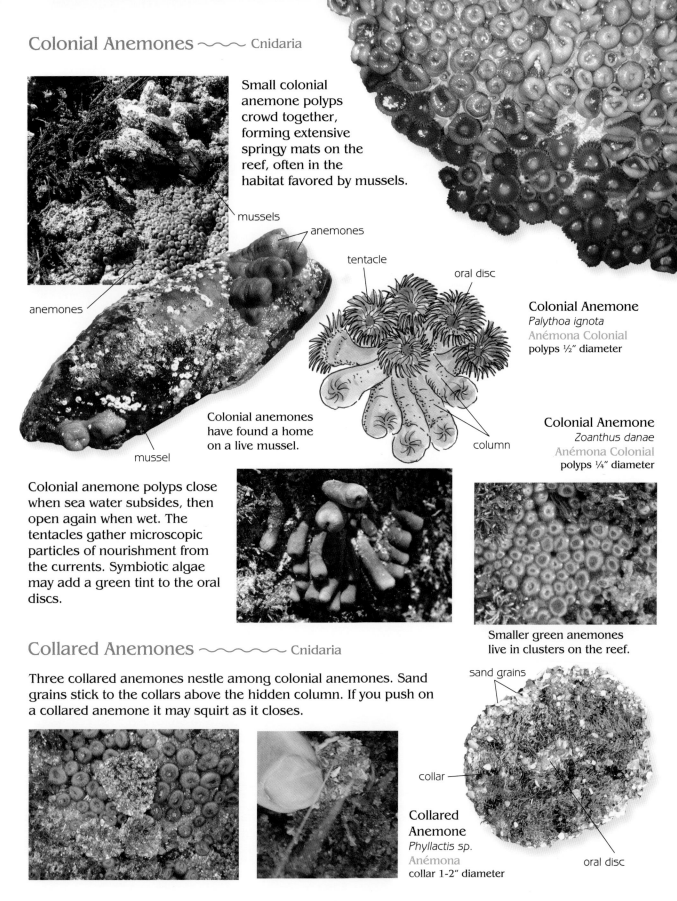

Small colonial anemone polyps crowd together, forming extensive springy mats on the reef, often in the habitat favored by mussels.

mussels

anemones

anemones

tentacle

oral disc

Colonial Anemone
Palythoa ignota
Anémona Colonial
polyps ½" diameter

Colonial anemones have found a home on a live mussel.

mussel

column

Colonial Anemone
Zoanthus danae
Anémona Colonial
polyps ¼" diameter

Colonial anemone polyps close when sea water subsides, then open again when wet. The tentacles gather microscopic particles of nourishment from the currents. Symbiotic algae may add a green tint to the oral discs.

Smaller green anemones live in clusters on the reef.

Collared Anemones ～～～ Cnidaria

Three collared anemones nestle among colonial anemones. Sand grains stick to the collars above the hidden column. If you push on a collared anemone it may squirt as it closes.

sand grains

collar

Collared Anemone
Phyllactis sp.
Anémona
collar 1-2" diameter

oral disc

Sea Anemones

Cnidaria

Warty Anemone
Bunodosoma californica
Anémona
column to 3" high
oral disc 1½-3" diameter

Do anemones have enemies?

Yes, but not very many. Most small marine animals are more likely to be eaten by an anemone than to eat one. Certain sea slugs, nudibranchs and some fish are immune to the paralyzing stings of anemone tentacles and dare to feed on this beautiful but poisonous creature. Unfortunately, human beings head the list of anemones' enemies due to pollution, accidental or intentional destruction of habitat and even malicious mischief by visitors to the beach.

The pedal disc of a warty anemone attaches firmly to an overhanging ledge above or into the substrate below. The body contracts and expands as tides ebb and swell. The anemone conserves water by closing its oral disc at low tide, then opening up and extending its tentacles as the sea water returns.

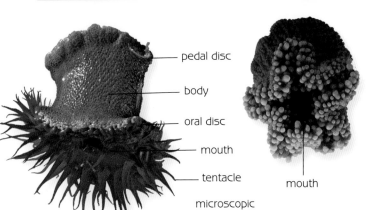

- pedal disc
- body
- oral disc
- mouth
- tentacle
- microscopic
- nematocyst

mouth

The mouth of an anemone is surrounded by tentacles tipped with microscopic stinging cells (nematocysts). Nematocysts discharge a venomous liquid to stun food passing by. The tentacles must then maneuver the prey into the anemone's waiting mouth.

An anemone has a very basic digestive system with a mouth on the oral surface connected to a simple gut called the coelenteron. The opposite (aboral) surface has no anal pass-through exit, so undigested bits of food are regurgitated back out of the mouth.

Warty anemones are carnivorous (flesh-eating) animals of two types: predators and particle-feeders:

Predatory anemones feed on shrimp, crabs, clams, mussels or fish that get trapped in their tentacles. They are adept at consuming animals larger than themselves.

Particle-feeding anemones catch microscopic larvae or free-floating plankton drifting past on the tide or on currents they create by waving their own tentacles.

The Mexican warty anemone has parallel rows of warts evenly spaced around its entire body. The warts covering most anemone bodies are spaced randomly and are tightly packed but flexible.

Mexican Warty Anemone
Western Flyer Anemone
Isoaulactinia hespervolita
Anémona Mexicana
column 2-2½" high
oral disc 2½" diameter

anemone waiting for food

particle-feeding anemone

Gorgonians ～～～～～ Cnidaria

Gorgonians are colonial cnidarians, related to sea anemones, hydroids and corals. They branch from a trunk-like holdfast attached to the substrate. Some species look like trees; others look like fans.

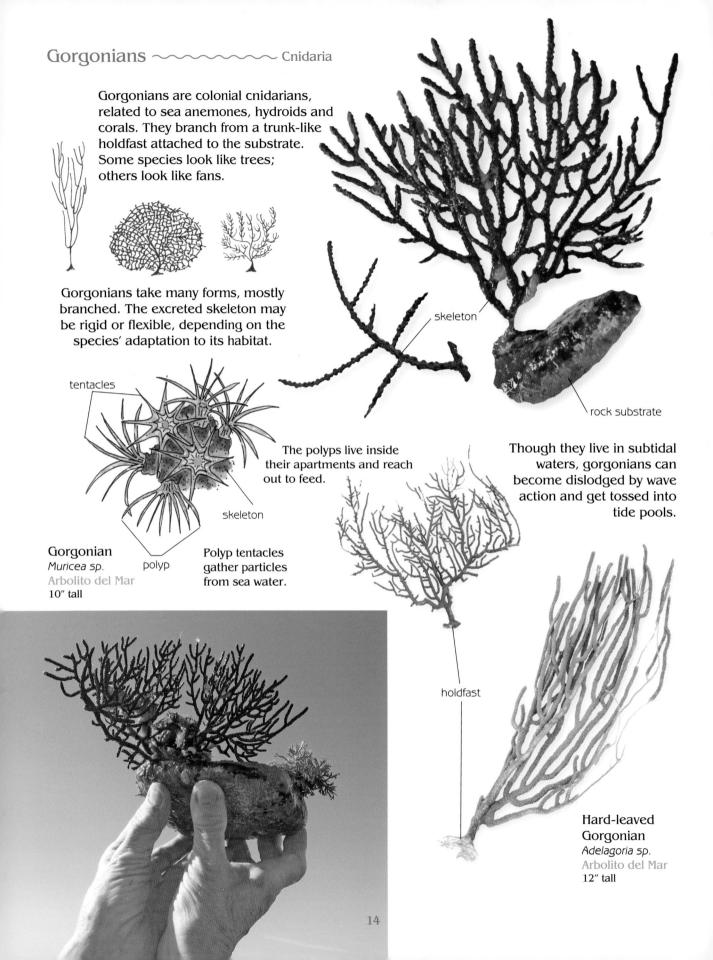

Gorgonians take many forms, mostly branched. The excreted skeleton may be rigid or flexible, depending on the species' adaptation to its habitat.

tentacles

skeleton

The polyps live inside their apartments and reach out to feed.

Gorgonian
Muricea sp.
Arbolito del Mar
10" tall

polyp

Polyp tentacles gather particles from sea water.

skeleton

rock substrate

Though they live in subtidal waters, gorgonians can become dislodged by wave action and get tossed into tide pools.

holdfast

Hard-leaved Gorgonian
Adelagoria sp.
Arbolito del Mar
12" tall

Hydroids
∼ Cnidaria ∼

Cnidarian hydroids are plumes of tentacles with microscopic stinging nematocysts on the tips. They feed on small crustaceans, using the nematocysts to immobilize their prey. Many tiny polyps and distinctive brown rice-like grains (corbulae) grow on branches of ostrich plume hydroids. The corbulae release eggs or sperm for reproduction.

corbulae

microscopic nematocysts on ends of tentacles

Ostrich Plume Hydroid
Aglaophenia diegensis
Hydroide
4-6" high

These innocent looking feather-like critters have been called powerful stinging beasts. Be careful!

Stinging Hydroid
Macrohynchia philippina
Hydroide
branches to 1"

Branching colonies of individual polyps form clumps of silvery stinging hydroids sometimes covering several yards of substrate. Hydroids reproduce sexually; they release eggs and sperm that settle nearby as larvae to strengthen and enlarge the parental colony. These larvae become tiny jellies (hydromedusae) that eventually swim away and form new hydroid colonies elsewhere.

Jellies
∼ Cnidaria

Jellies (formerly called jellyfish) are deep water cnidarians, related to hydroids, with nematocysts on their tentacles. The Portuguese man-of-war has a gas-filled float that keeps its body on top of the water with stinging tentacles trailing along behind. When small animals or fish get caught in its tentacles, they are stung, paralyzed and eaten.

In summer, jellies are carried in to shore by winds and currents. Accidental contact with jellies in the water may cause serious stings and possibly severe allergic reactions in swimmers or tidewalkers.

Photo by Alex Kerstitch

Avoid touching or stepping on hydroids or jellies on the beach. Their stings can be painful even after they are dried up or dead!

Portuguese Man-of-War
Physalia utriculus
Aguamala
float 2-3" long

Coral Porites
∼ Cnidaria

Emerald Coral Porite
Porites panamensis
Coral Verde
colonies 3-5" thick
12-20" across

Encrusting coral porites are the only true corals found in the upper Gulf. Further south, colonies join together to form reefs, but cold water temperatures limit reef-building in the north.

live specimen

dead skeleton

individual polyps

Flatworms ~~~~~~~~ Platyhelminthes

Flatworms are primitive, carnivorous bottom dwellers that may be found gliding across rock surfaces or crawling in sand or mud under rocks and algae. They may appear as slimy, gelatinous blobs, or as flat leaf-like shapes stretched long and narrow as they slither across basalt boulders. In open water, they spread a peripheral ruffle as they undulate through the sea. They are so thin they do not need a circulatory system.

Speckled Flatworm
Pseudoceros bajae
Gusano Plano
1-2" long

Brown Speckled Flatworm
Pseudoceros sp.
Gusano Plano
1-2" long

Dorid Nudibranch

A flatworm's coloration varies with its diet of microscopic organisms, sea squirts, segmented worms, eel grass, mussel eggs or other live prey.

The coloration of some speckled flatworms is believed to involve mimicry, a biological survival mechanism whereby one species evolves to resemble another—in this case the dorid nudibranch mimicking a speckled flatworm. Mimicry serves to warn potential predators of distasteful or toxic chemicals carried in flatworms that might also be present in the nudibranch.

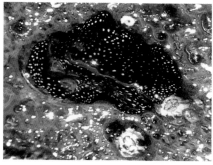

Mexican Flatworm
Pseudoceros mexicanus
Gusano Plano
1-3" long

The Mexican flatworm is sometimes called the Mexican skirt dancer.

Tidewalkers should exercise extreme care in handling flatworms. Although flatworms do not sting or bite, their bodies are soft and fragile. They are so delicate that they can even tear or injure themselves while moving over sharp terrain. Marine biologists study flatworms because of their amazing powers of rapid regeneration and recovery.

This beautiful flatworm is slightly larger than the speckled flatworm and has a reddish-orange band around its ruffled margin.

Segmented Worms ～～～ Annelida

Annelid (many-segmented) worms are found on rocky, sandy and muddy shores and at all depths of the sea. They have definite heads with eyes, and a simple digestive system running their entire length from mouth to anus. They also have acute senses of touch and taste.

head

parapodia

Segmented Sand Worm
Phyllodoce tuberculosa
Gusano Areñoso
to 8" long

anus

Do you see the brittle stars?

Mexican Fireworm
Eurythoe complanata
Gusano de Fuego
4-6" long

head

Appendages called parapodia (lateral feet) extend from both sides along the bodies of segmented worms. Parapodia carry both bristles and lobes that serve as locomotive paddles, allowing the worm to swim freely in the sea or hurry across the sand and burrow quickly out of danger.

Many marine worms have an extraordinary ability to extend or retract their bodies comparatively great distances in search of food. It is fascinating to watch them inching along on the surface of the sand.

Handle with care! Fireworms can inflict painful stings when calcium carbonate spines dislodge into your skin!

Ribbon Worms ～～～ Nemertea

proboscis

Non-segmented nemertean ribbon worms are carnivorous predators found under rocks, algae or soft sand. They hunt with their proboscis, using it to wrap around or to inject toxins into their prey.

Amphitrite Medusa Worm
Sabellidae sp.
The polychaete medusa worm has a long body burrowing deep into the substrate. It spreads its bright red branchial plumes (fine tentacles) like a net over the surface of the reef, gathering organic food bits to pass into the mouth.

Ribbon Worm
Anopla sp.
Gusano Cinta
to 6" long

Ribbon Worm
Anopla sp.
Gusano Cinta
4-6" long

17

Tube Worms ~~~~~~~~~~~~~~~~ Annelida

Marine polychaete (many-bristled) worms have two life-styles: unattached or living in a tube. Tube-dweller species use a variety of material and methods to build their homes. When the tide comes in, tube worms extend their tentacles and filter the water for food that drifts by.

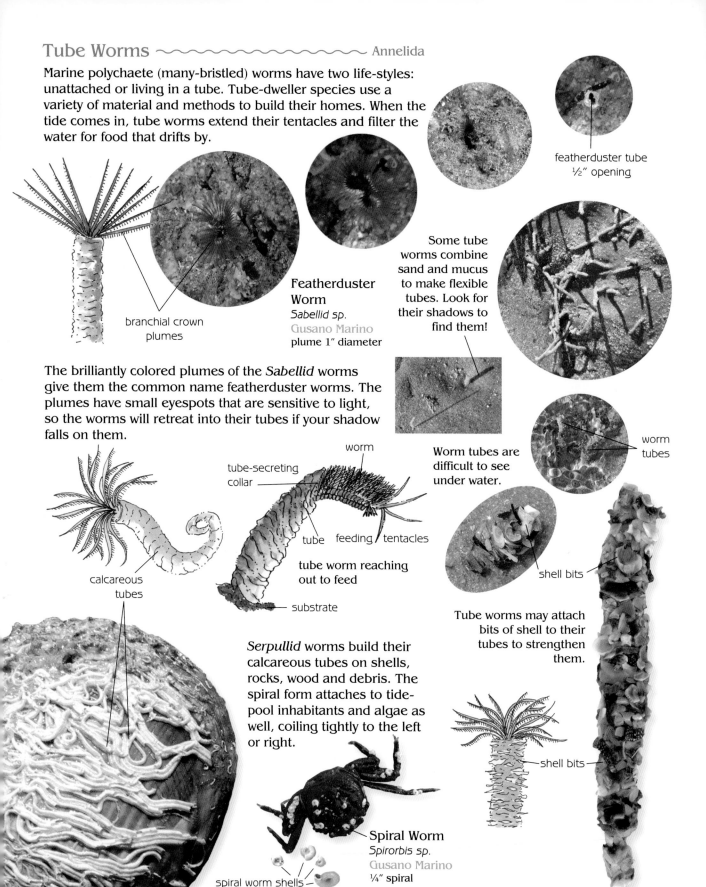

featherduster tube
½" opening

branchial crown
plumes

Featherduster Worm
Sabellid sp.
Gusano Marino
plume 1" diameter

Some tube worms combine sand and mucus to make flexible tubes. Look for their shadows to find them!

The brilliantly colored plumes of the *Sabellid* worms give them the common name featherduster worms. The plumes have small eyespots that are sensitive to light, so the worms will retreat into their tubes if your shadow falls on them.

calcareous tubes

tube-secreting collar

worm

tube   feeding tentacles

tube worm reaching out to feed

substrate

Worm tubes are difficult to see under water.

worm tubes

shell bits

Tube worms may attach bits of shell to their tubes to strengthen them.

Serpullid worms build their calcareous tubes on shells, rocks, wood and debris. The spiral form attaches to tide-pool inhabitants and algae as well, coiling tightly to the left or right.

shell bits

spiral worm shells

Spiral Worm
Spirorbis sp.
Gusano Marino
¼" spiral

18

Chitons ~~~~~~~~~~~~~~~ Polyplacophora

The chiton, a primitive mollusc, is well suited to the rigors of life on the rocky coast. Eight separate overlapping plates protect its body and provide the flexibility the chiton needs to cling to uneven rocks. A negative-pressure seal and glue-like secretions help the chiton avoid being swept away by the surf or pried off by curious tidewalkers.

When dislodged, chitons roll into protective balls.

Chiton
Stenoplax sp.
Quitón
to 2" long

A chiton lays eggs that will hatch out of their cases when mature.

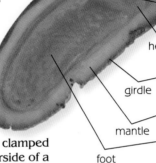

mouth and radula
gills
head
girdle
mantle
foot
ventral surface

This chiton clamped to the underside of a reef rock when the tide went out.

Most chiton species are herbivores—they use their radula to scrape algae off the rocks.

Chitons are also called sea cradles or coat-of-mail snails.

plate
girdle has alternating stripes

The mantle and its thick edge, the girdle, hold the plates together. Contractions move the chiton along as it competes with its neighbors for space and food.

Striped Chiton
Chiton virgulatus
Quitón
2-4" long

Oysters 〰️〰️〰️〰️〰️〰️ Mollusca

Oysters in the upper Gulf attach to hard substrates and cluster in mud. Masses of them form cliffs when larvae settle onto older oysters again and again. The cliffs provide habitat for fish, barnacles, anemones and other intertidal residents. Oysters can even be found on sandy shores on scattered basalt and granite rocks.

Blue Rock Oyster, Palm Oyster
Saccostrea palmula
Ostra de Palma
to 2½" long

native oyster

commercial oyster

The oyster's bottom valve conforms to the underlying surface and makes a fringed cup for the top valve, protecting the animal inside. Oysters filter food from the water currents and are known to remove toxic matter from the sea.

Native oysters at low tide on a Gulf estero shore

Local communities grow commercial species in several Gulf esteros. This labor-intensive culture depends on daily tidal flow to bring food to the oysters and requires constant tending by the farmers to produce a viable harvest. Careful monitoring is essential to protect the crop and the health of the estero.

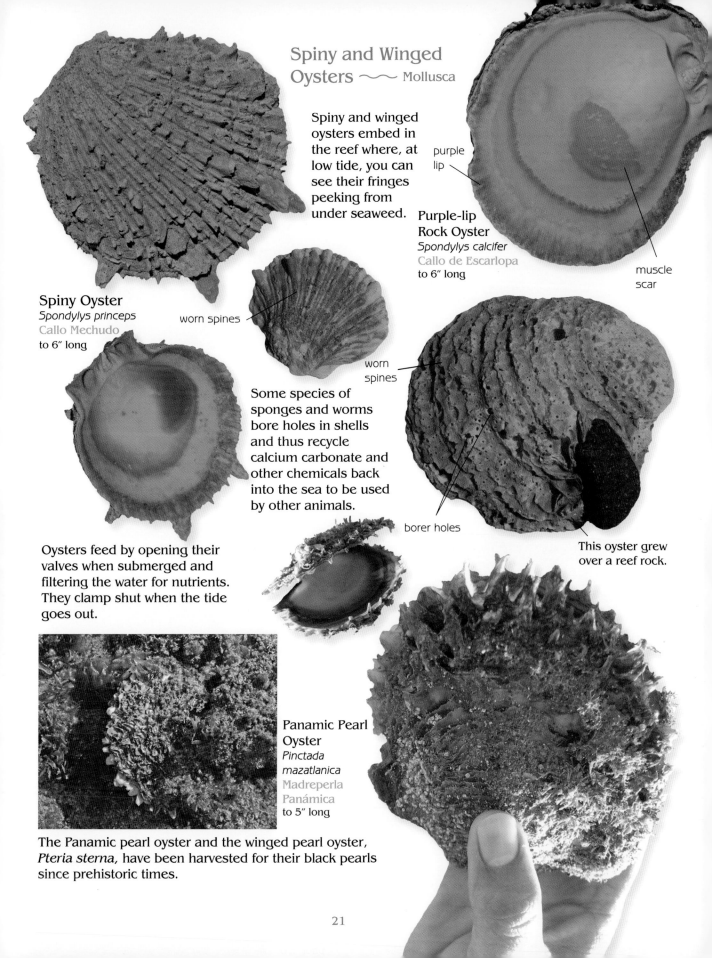

Spiny and Winged Oysters ～ Mollusca

Spiny and winged oysters embed in the reef where, at low tide, you can see their fringes peeking from under seaweed.

purple lip

muscle scar

Purple-lip Rock Oyster
Spondylys calcifer
Callo de Escarlopa
to 6" long

Spiny Oyster
Spondylys princeps
Callo Mechudo
to 6" long

worn spines

worn spines

Some species of sponges and worms bore holes in shells and thus recycle calcium carbonate and other chemicals back into the sea to be used by other animals.

borer holes

This oyster grew over a reef rock.

Oysters feed by opening their valves when submerged and filtering the water for nutrients. They clamp shut when the tide goes out.

Panamic Pearl Oyster
Pinctada mazatlanica
Madreperla Panámica
to 5" long

The Panamic pearl oyster and the winged pearl oyster, *Pteria sterna*, have been harvested for their black pearls since prehistoric times.

21

Jewel Box ～～～ Mollusca

Jewel Box
Chama sp.
Almeja
to 3½" wide

valve
fragment

hinge

The jewel box
bivalve is easily
overlooked because
it is often covered with
algae and other growths.
The lower valve attaches to
the substrate and is larger
than the flatter upper valve.

Perhaps this odd shell is called
a jewel box because it looks like
a container with a lid. Chama is
pronounced "kah-ma."

Swimming File Clam ～～～ Mollusca

The swimming file clam
uses byssal threads to
attach to the under-
side of a rock but is
easily dislodged if the
rock is turned over.
It swims backwards
by snapping its valves
together. Sticky tentacles
and the large mantle
are visible even
when the shell
is closed. The
swimming file
clam filters
food from the
water.

tentacles

siphon

Swimming File Clam
Limaria pacifica
Almeja
to 1½" wide

Mussels and Arks 〰〰 Mollusca

Mussels and arks are sessile (immobile) intertidal bivalves. They are difficult to recognize as living organisms because they appear to be part of the reef. They filter food from sea water.

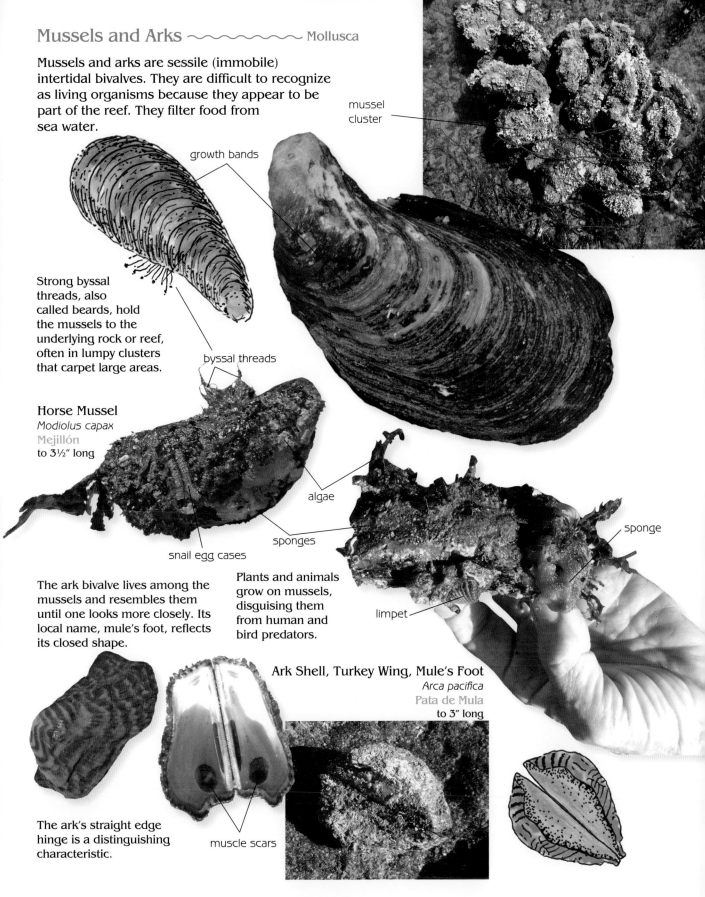

mussel cluster

growth bands

Strong byssal threads, also called beards, hold the mussels to the underlying rock or reef, often in lumpy clusters that carpet large areas.

byssal threads

Horse Mussel
Modiolus capax
Mejillón
to 3½" long

algae

sponges

snail egg cases

The ark bivalve lives among the mussels and resembles them until one looks more closely. Its local name, mule's foot, reflects its closed shape.

Plants and animals grow on mussels, disguising them from human and bird predators.

sponge

limpet

Ark Shell, Turkey Wing, Mule's Foot
Arca pacifica
Pata de Mula
to 3" long

The ark's straight edge hinge is a distinguishing characteristic.

muscle scars

23

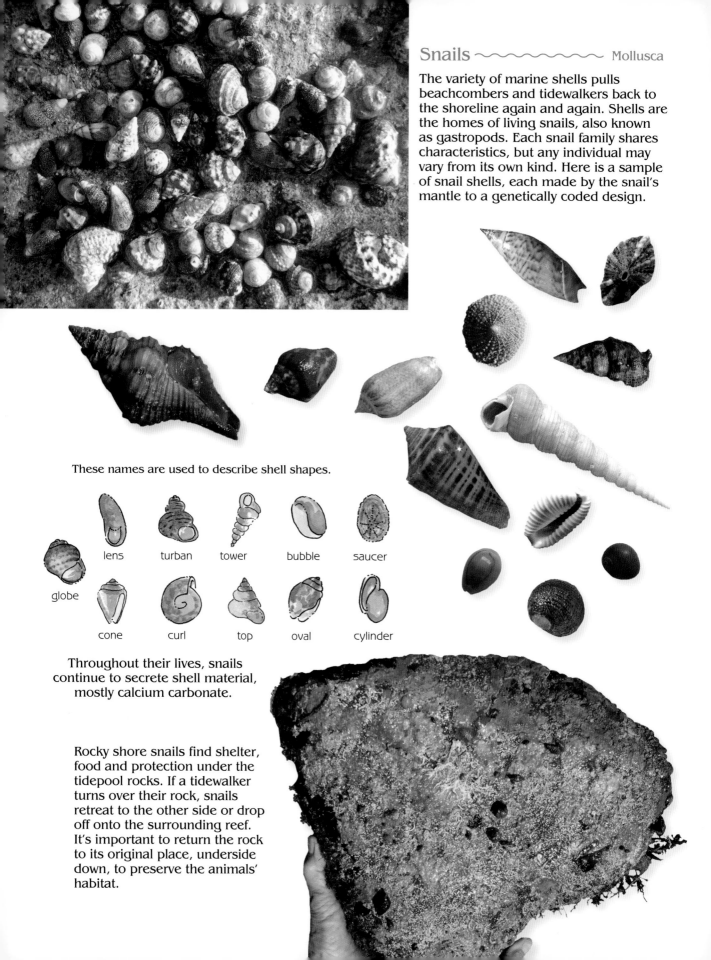

Snails ～～～～～～～ Mollusca

The variety of marine shells pulls beachcombers and tidewalkers back to the shoreline again and again. Shells are the homes of living snails, also known as gastropods. Each snail family shares characteristics, but any individual may vary from its own kind. Here is a sample of snail shells, each made by the snail's mantle to a genetically coded design.

These names are used to describe shell shapes.

globe   lens   turban   tower   bubble   saucer

cone   curl   top   oval   cylinder

Throughout their lives, snails continue to secrete shell material, mostly calcium carbonate.

Rocky shore snails find shelter, food and protection under the tidepool rocks. If a tidewalker turns over their rock, snails retreat to the other side or drop off onto the surrounding reef. It's important to return the rock to its original place, underside down, to preserve the animals' habitat.

Turban Snails ～～～～ Mollusca

Turban snails are one of the most common intertidal rocky shore species of the upper Gulf. Turbans glide across the reef feeding on algae.

operculum

The turban snail leaves its shell by folding the operculum out of the way.

top

bottom

Turban Snail
Turbo fluctuosus
Caracol Turbano
to 2″ high

The operculum is attached to the snail and when drawn shut protects the snail by discouraging predators and preventing moisture loss at low tide. Turban snail "doors" are round and hard like buttons. They are found on the beach after the snails die.

How snails eat

The radula is the eating part of a marine snail. A ribbon of moving sharp teeth scrapes algae off the reef or pierces prey and then pulls the food into the mouth. Mucus lubricates the conveyor-belt action and sticks particles together for easy passage to the stomach. New teeth constantly replace worn ones.

siphon

radula tooth

proboscis

foot

Besides its scraping action, the radula can be extended to drill into a prey's hard shell.

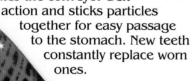

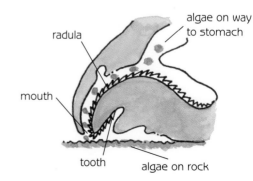

algae on way to stomach

radula

mouth

tooth

algae on rock

Cone Snail
Conus sp.
Caracol Cono
to 2″ high

A cone snail can inject venom into prey (or your hand!) with a thrust of its harpoon-like tooth.

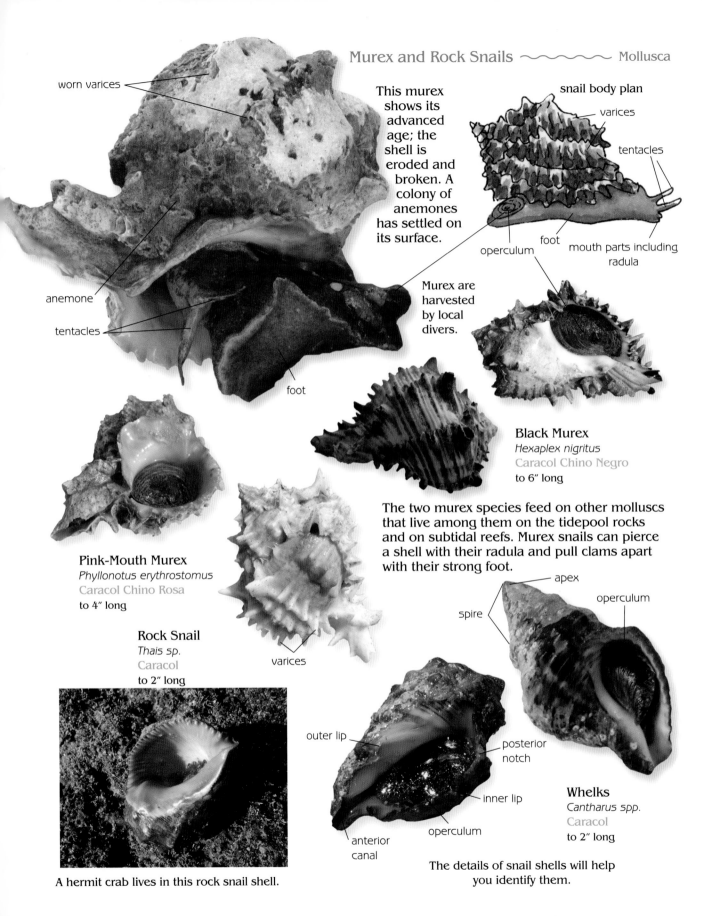

worn varices

This murex shows its advanced age; the shell is eroded and broken. A colony of anemones has settled on its surface.

snail body plan

varices

tentacles

operculum

foot

mouth parts including radula

anemone

tentacles

foot

Murex are harvested by local divers.

Black Murex
Hexaplex nigritus
Caracol Chino Negro
to 6" long

Pink-Mouth Murex
Phyllonotus erythrostomus
Caracol Chino Rosa
to 4" long

Rock Snail
Thais sp.
Caracol
to 2" long

varices

The two murex species feed on other molluscs that live among them on the tidepool rocks and on subtidal reefs. Murex snails can pierce a shell with their radula and pull clams apart with their strong foot.

apex

spire

operculum

outer lip

posterior notch

inner lip

operculum

anterior canal

Whelks
Cantharus spp.
Caracol
to 2" long

A hermit crab lives in this rock snail shell.

The details of snail shells will help you identify them.

Olives and Small Snails ～～ Mollusca

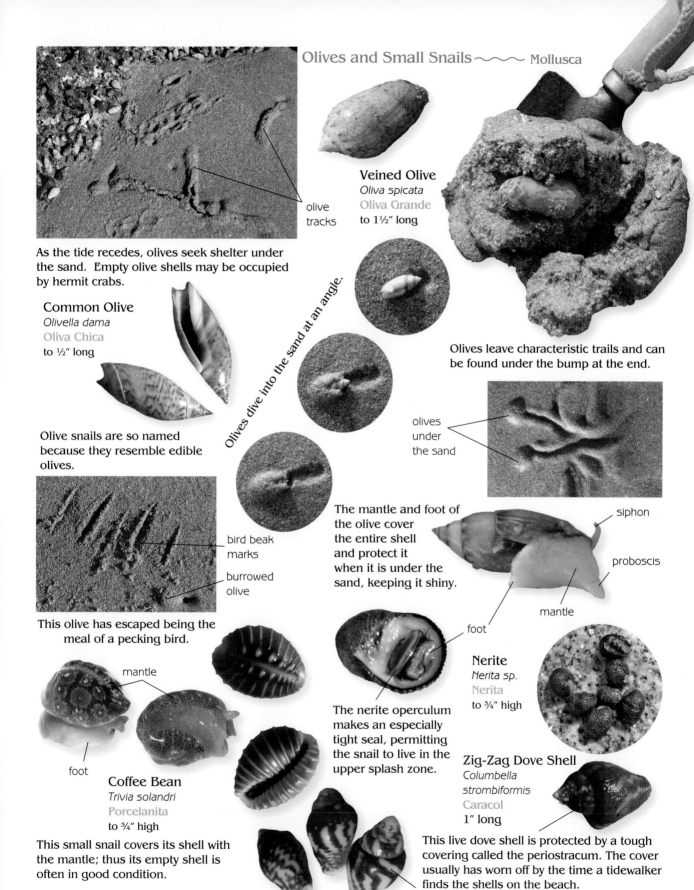

olive tracks

As the tide recedes, olives seek shelter under the sand. Empty olive shells may be occupied by hermit crabs.

Veined Olive
Oliva spicata
Oliva Grande
to 1½" long

Olives leave characteristic trails and can be found under the bump at the end.

Common Olive
Olivella dama
Oliva Chica
to ½" long

Olive snails are so named because they resemble edible olives.

Olives dive into the sand at an angle.

olives under the sand

bird beak marks

burrowed olive

This olive has escaped being the meal of a pecking bird.

The mantle and foot of the olive cover the entire shell and protect it when it is under the sand, keeping it shiny.

siphon

proboscis

mantle

foot

mantle

foot

Coffee Bean
Trivia solandri
Porcelanita
to ¾" high

This small snail covers its shell with the mantle; thus its empty shell is often in good condition.

The nerite operculum makes an especially tight seal, permitting the snail to live in the upper splash zone.

Nerite
Nerita sp.
Nerita
to ¾" high

Zig-Zag Dove Shell
Columbella strombiformis
Caracol
1" long

This live dove shell is protected by a tough covering called the periostracum. The cover usually has worn off by the time a tidewalker finds the shells on the beach.

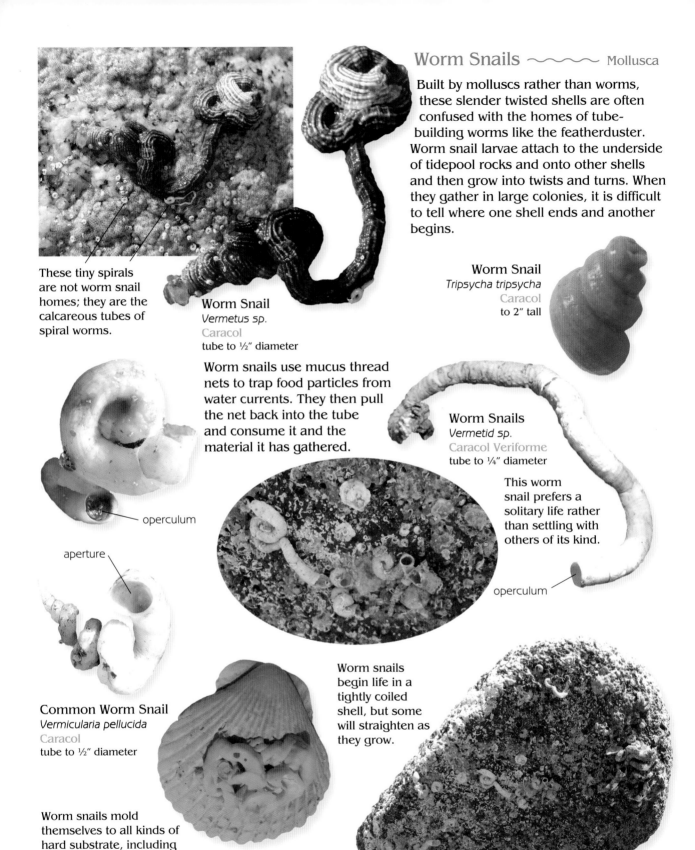

Worm Snails ～～～ Mollusca

Built by molluscs rather than worms, these slender twisted shells are often confused with the homes of tube-building worms like the featherduster. Worm snail larvae attach to the underside of tidepool rocks and onto other shells and then grow into twists and turns. When they gather in large colonies, it is difficult to tell where one shell ends and another begins.

These tiny spirals are not worm snail homes; they are the calcareous tubes of spiral worms.

Worm Snail
Vermetus sp.
Caracol
tube to ½" diameter

Worm Snail
Tripsycha tripsycha
Caracol
to 2" tall

Worm snails use mucus thread nets to trap food particles from water currents. They then pull the net back into the tube and consume it and the material it has gathered.

Worm Snails
Vermetid sp.
Caracol Veriforme
tube to ¼" diameter

This worm snail prefers a solitary life rather than settling with others of its kind.

operculum

aperture

operculum

Common Worm Snail
Vermicularia pellucida
Caracol
tube to ½" diameter

Worm snails begin life in a tightly coiled shell, but some will straighten as they grow.

Worm snails mold themselves to all kinds of hard substrate, including rocks and shells.

Limpets, Cup and Saucers and Slipper Shells
Mollusca

Limpets, cup and saucer shells and slipper shells adhere to rocks, seaweeds and other molluscs. Their shells display many textures and colors as well as variations on the cone shape.

mantle

The keyhole limpet has a hole in its apex. It can pull its large mantle under its shell.

Some limpets have a protective covering of hair-like scales called a periostracum that helps to disguise them while they graze on algae.

mouth and radula
head
mantle
shell
foot

ventral surface

Keyhole Limpet
Diadora inequalis
Lapa
to 1½" long

Slipper Shell
Crepidula sp.
Lapa
to 1" long

The pocket gives the shell its slipper-like appearance.

Chinese Hat Limpet
Calyptraea mamillaris
Lapa
to 1¼" long

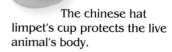

The chinese hat limpet's cup protects the live animal's body.

cup

saucer

Spiny Cup and Saucer
Crucibulum spinosum
Lapa Espinosa
to 1" long

Can you find the six limpets that have settled onto this granite rock?

limpet home scars on the reef

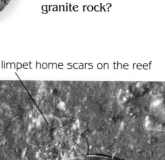

Panamic Horse Hoof Limpet
Hipponix panamensis
Lapa
to 1½" long

Stanford Limpet
Lottia stanfordiana
Lapa
to 1" long

Limpets scrape algae off the rocks with the radula. Limpets may return to their starting place at night and settle onto a home scar that provides a secreted ridge for better suction.

Snails and Their Opercula

Cerith

Rock Snail

Worm Snail

Pink Murex

Nerite

Turban

Cerith

Pink Mouth Murex

Turban

Moon Snail

Moon Snail

Whelk and Egg Cases

Turban Snail

Black Murex

Top Snail

Turban

Melongena

Oyster Drill

Opercula

An operculum is the horny or calcareous plate that acts as a door, lid or shield for a univalve mollusc when the snail withdraws into its shell. A powerful ligament extends or contracts to open or close the door. This action can be very rapid when danger threatens or slow and tentative when the snail is cautiously exploring its environment.

Opercula come in many shapes and sizes, according to the openings they cover.

Pink Mouth Murex
Phyllonotus erythrostomus
Caracol China Rosa
to 4" long

A murex operculum is rough on the outer surface and smooth inside. It is larger than most opercula because the mouth (aperture) of the shell must accommodate the movements of the comparatively large snail inside.

Cortez Melongena
Melongena patula
Caracol Melon
to 4" high

Cortez melongenas' claw-like opercula are elongated ovals pointed at one end. They are used in defense and locomotion by this pear-shaped member of the whelk family.

interior surface   exterior surface

Button-like, spiral opercula of turban snails are often found by tidewalkers on beaches of the northern Gulf.

Moon Snail
Polinices sp.
Caracol de Luna
1" diameter

The operculum of a top snail looks like an almost perfect circle.

Top Snail
Tegula corteziana
height to ½"

Turban Snail
Turbo fluctuosus
Caracol Turbano
to 2" high

The ovate operculum of a moon snail is smooth and glossy on both sides.

A worm snail's operculum is cone-shaped like a rubber bathtub plug for water control during tidal changes.

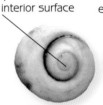

Worm Snail
Vermetid sp.
Caracol Veriforme
tube to ¼" diameter

Cone Snail
Conus sp.
Caracol Cono
to 2" high

The poisonous cone snail has a long narrow operculum to match the narrow slit of its mouth.

Sea Hares ～～～～ Mollusca

Sea hares are snails without visible shells. They are called sea hares because of the two rhinophores located just above the eyes that resemble rabbit ears. However, rhinophores are organs for smelling rather than hearing.

California Sea Hare
Aplysia californica
Liebre del Mar
to 24" long

rhinophores

black sea hare burrowed in sand

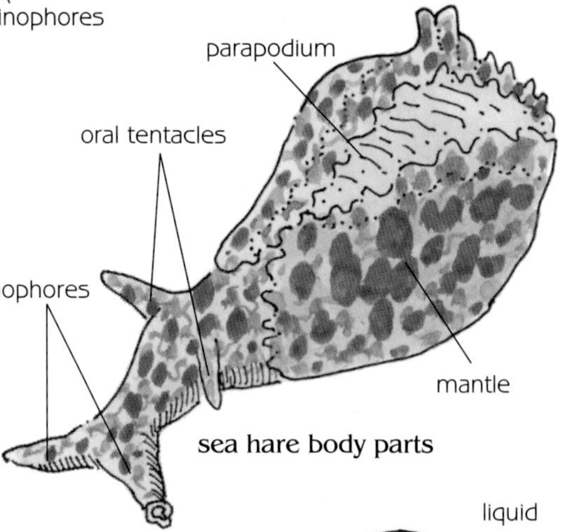

parapodium

oral tentacles

rhinophores

mantle

sea hare body parts

Black Sea Hare
Aplysia vaccaria
Liebre del Mar
to 10" long

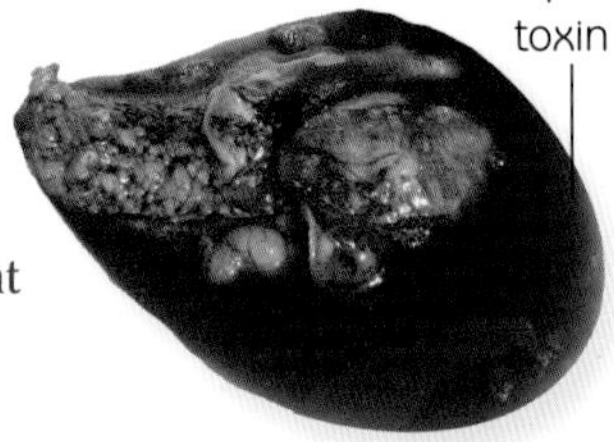

Sea hares graze on algae and seaweeds. They resemble small rocks, but when you touch a sea hare you know why it is described as jelly-bodied.

liquid toxin

When disturbed, sea hares may squirt a liquid that is toxic to some animals.

Sea hares can act as both males and females. This black sea hare has joined others in a mating chain to lay masses of eggs in strings that look like spaghetti.

egg strings

Black sea hares are unique to the northern Gulf.

32

Sea Slugs 〜〜〜〜 Mollusca

Sea slugs move upon the rocks using contractions that pull them forward on a muscular foot. Although they appear defenseless, some sea slugs can secrete toxic substances that deter predators. Some are brightly colored, which may warn predators to stay away. Others look so much like the surrounding habitat that they are difficult to see.

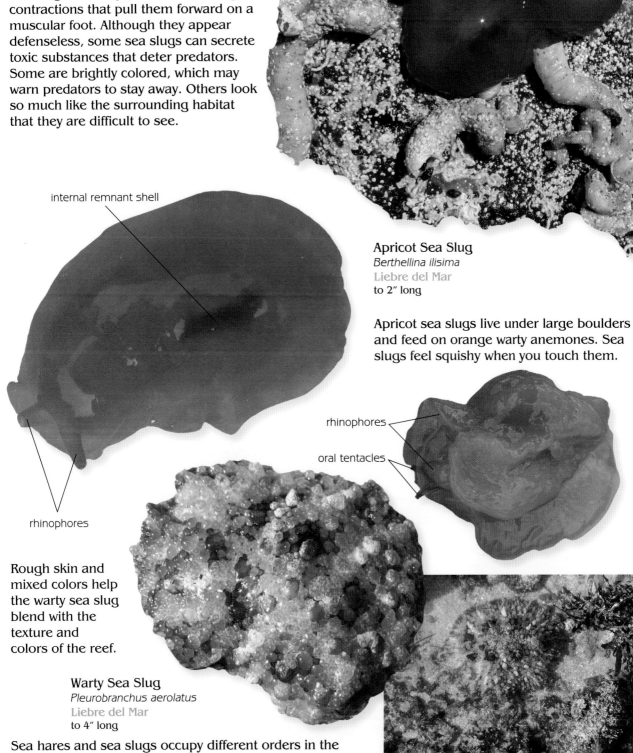

internal remnant shell

rhinophores

rhinophores

oral tentacles

Apricot Sea Slug
Berthellina ilisima
Liebre del Mar
to 2" long

Apricot sea slugs live under large boulders and feed on orange warty anemones. Sea slugs feel squishy when you touch them.

Rough skin and mixed colors help the warty sea slug blend with the texture and colors of the reef.

Warty Sea Slug
Pleurobranchus aerolatus
Liebre del Mar
to 4" long

Sea hares and sea slugs occupy different orders in the subclass opisthobranchia, which also includes nudibranchs. As they have evolved, these molluscs have lost their outer shells.

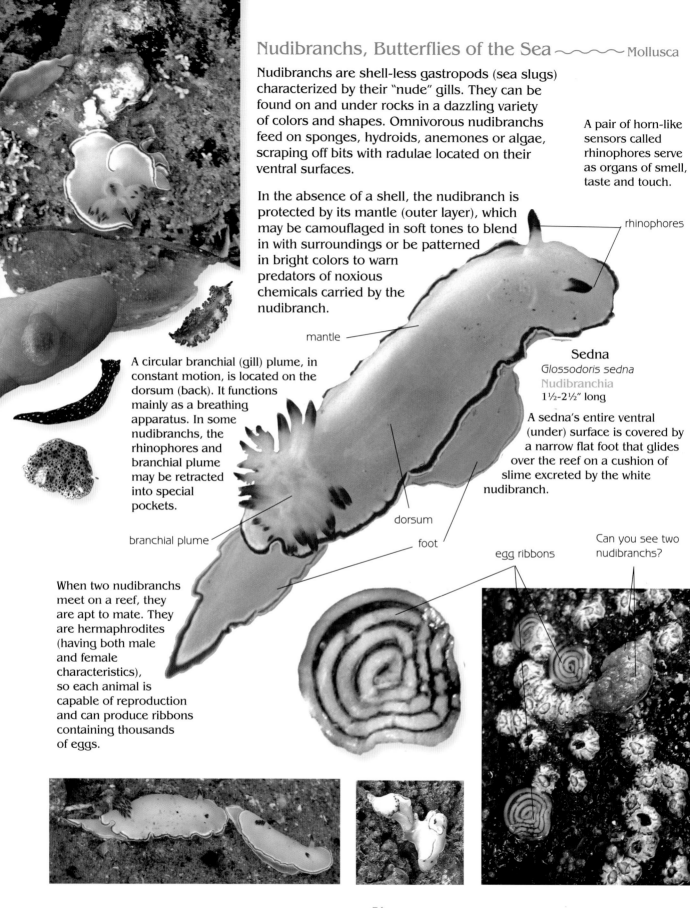

Nudibranchs, Butterflies of the Sea ~~~ Mollusca

Nudibranchs are shell-less gastropods (sea slugs) characterized by their "nude" gills. They can be found on and under rocks in a dazzling variety of colors and shapes. Omnivorous nudibranchs feed on sponges, hydroids, anemones or algae, scraping off bits with radulae located on their ventral surfaces.

A pair of horn-like sensors called rhinophores serve as organs of smell, taste and touch.

In the absence of a shell, the nudibranch is protected by its mantle (outer layer), which may be camouflaged in soft tones to blend in with surroundings or be patterned in bright colors to warn predators of noxious chemicals carried by the nudibranch.

rhinophores

mantle

Sedna
Glossodoris sedna
Nudibranchia
1½-2½" long

A circular branchial (gill) plume, in constant motion, is located on the dorsum (back). It functions mainly as a breathing apparatus. In some nudibranchs, the rhinophores and branchial plume may be retracted into special pockets.

A sedna's entire ventral (under) surface is covered by a narrow flat foot that glides over the reef on a cushion of slime excreted by the white nudibranch.

branchial plume

dorsum

foot

egg ribbons

Can you see two nudibranchs?

When two nudibranchs meet on a reef, they are apt to mate. They are hermaphrodites (having both male and female characteristics), so each animal is capable of reproduction and can produce ribbons containing thousands of eggs.

Nudibranchs ~~~~ Mollusca

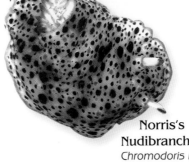

Norris's Nudibranch
Chromodoris norrisi
Nudibranchia
1½-2½" long

Dall's Nudibranch
Glossodoris dalli
Nudibranchia
¾-1¾" long

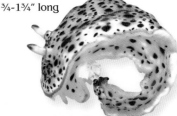

The colorful Dall's nudibranch resembles Norris's nudibranch but is somewhat smaller and lighter in color.

Tidewalkers may occasionally see nudibranchs cruising on an open expanse of tidepool sand, but they are usually found nearer their food sources on or under rocks and ledges in intertidal and subtidal habitats.

Longitudinal yellow and orange spots, interspersed with brilliant blue accents, adorn the dorsum and foot of the California nudibranch.

Mexican Dancer
Elysia diomedea
Bailador Mexicano
1½-2½" long

margin

California Chromodorid
Hypselodoris californiensis
Nudibranchia
1½-2½" long

rhinophores

The pale yellowish green of the Mexican dancer derives from chloroplasts (photosynthetic cells) in its tissues, due to its green algae diet. Yellow and black stripes line its distinctive rhinophores, and its frilly margins are a variegated mixture of purple, orange and pale blue.

Knobby Aeolid
Limenandra nodosa
Nudibranchia
1-2½" long

Spindle-shaped cerata cover the dorsal surface of this aeolid nudibranch. It glides across the reef looking for hydroids or anemones to munch.

cerata

Undeterred by the protective nematocysts (stinging cells) of its anemone prey, the knobby aeolid ingests and transforms the nematocysts into special stinging cells of its own called cnidosacs.

Nudibranchs have developed complex defense mechanisms against predators, including toxic secretions that smell and taste repugnant to their enemies. Other animal species mimic nudibranchs using bright coloration as a warning to discourage potential attackers.

Octopuses ～～～～～ Mollusca

Octopuses* are predators of the class of animals called cephalopods, meaning head-footed. This agile mollusc moves smoothly and swiftly as it hunts for snails, crabs and fish to eat. Eight strong arms equipped with double rows of suction cups help the octopus grab and hold onto its prey. The octopus both tastes and feels what it touches.

Octopuses are creatures of the sea that are known for their intelligence and adaptability.

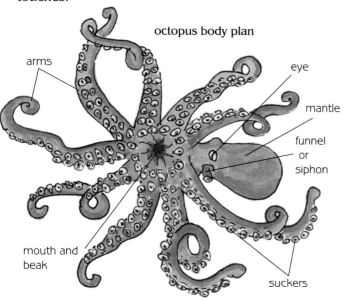

octopus body plan

arms

eye

mantle

funnel or siphon

mouth and beak

suckers

Fitch's Octopus
Octopus fitchi
Pulpito
head to 2" long,
arms to 3 times body
length

beak

mouth

Octopuses have very sharp beaks and may bite when handled. They inject venom from salivary glands. Octopuses also defend themselves by squirting ink and changing colors to match the substrate.

The octopus seeks shelter under rocks and in reef holes. It can squeeze into very small spaces because it has no skeleton.

A plastic dish is a good place for the octopus to rest while you observe it.

*Although you may hear these interesting creatures called octopi, the more accepted term is octopuses.

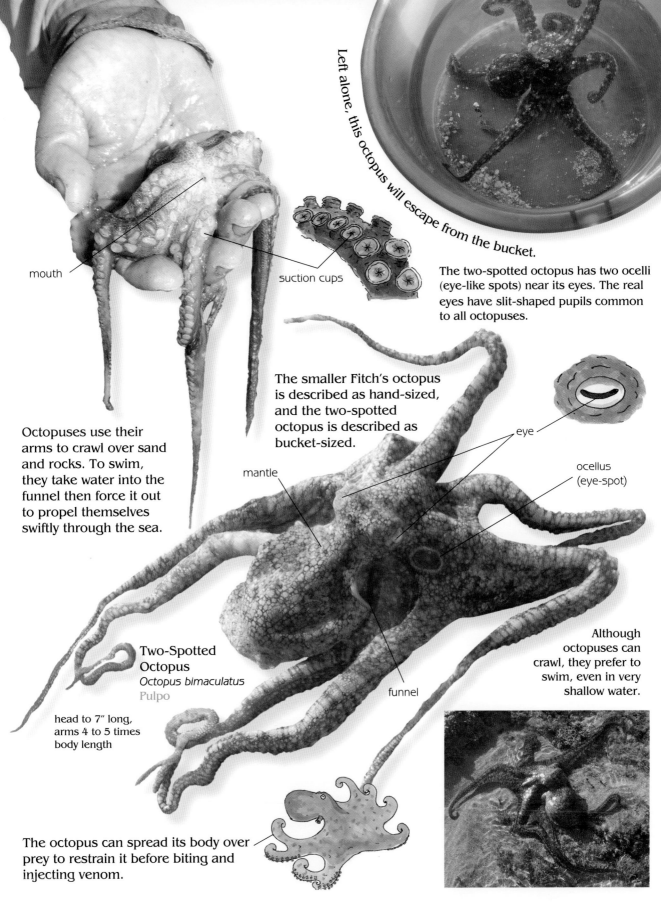

mouth

suction cups

Left alone, this octopus will escape from the bucket.

The two-spotted octopus has two ocelli (eye-like spots) near its eyes. The real eyes have slit-shaped pupils common to all octopuses.

The smaller Fitch's octopus is described as hand-sized, and the two-spotted octopus is described as bucket-sized.

mantle

eye

ocellus (eye-spot)

Octopuses use their arms to crawl over sand and rocks. To swim, they take water into the funnel then force it out to propel themselves swiftly through the sea.

Although octopuses can crawl, they prefer to swim, even in very shallow water.

Two-Spotted Octopus
Octopus bimaculatus
Pulpo

head to 7" long, arms 4 to 5 times body length

funnel

The octopus can spread its body over prey to restrain it before biting and injecting venom.

Shrimp 〜〜〜〜〜〜〜〜〜〜〜〜〜〜〜〜〜〜〜 Arthropoda

Tidepool shrimp belong to the crustecean subphyla and are smaller than commercially harvested shrimp. Most species search the tide pools for small organic particles and algae.

antenna

eye

tail

abdomen

snapping claw

carapace

small claw

snapping claw

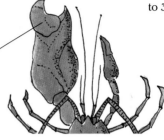

Pistol or Snapping Shrimp
Alpheus sp.
Camerón Pistola
to 3" long

The snapping or pistol shrimp uses its large claw to stun small fish and other prey by making a shock wave. As the claw closes, a jet of water stuns the prey and produces a "cavitation" bubble. The collapse of this bubble causes the snapping sound.

Scientists have observed that if the snapping claw is pulled off, the shimp will regrow it during the next molt but on the opposite side.

Shrimp snapping together produce a familiar tidepool chorus. You'll hear them before you see them.

This transparent shrimp is almost invisible.

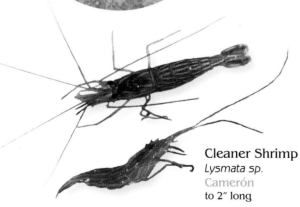

Cleaner Shrimp
Lysmata sp.
Camerón
to 2" long

Tidepool shrimp stir the sand for small organisms and other animals' leftovers. Some shrimp clean parasites from fish.

Four shrimp, a crab and a fish have been left high and dry by the receding tide. Can you find them?

Porcelain Crabs ~~~~~~ Arthropoda

Porcelain crabs have only three sets of developed walking legs, while regular crabs have four. These tiny crustaceans seek shelter in the beachrock and cling to the underside of boulders, eating organic matter that floats by. The Gulf is home to over twenty-five porcelain crab species. Several are endemic: they occur nowhere else.

Porcelain Crab
Petrolisthes gracilis
Cangrejo Porcelana
carapace 1" wide

three walking legs on each side

Porcelain Crab
Petrolisthes hirtipes
Cangrejo Porcelana
carapace ½" wide

Porcelain crabs are known for their ability to discard a limb when a predator grabs it. This process is called autotomy, which also serves to provide food to the predator, giving the little crab time to escape. During several moltings the missing part may regenerate.

walking legs

eggs

tubercles

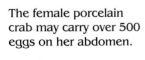

The female porcelain crab may carry over 500 eggs on her abdomen.

Hermit Crabs 〜 Arthropoda

Hermit crabs don't have their own shells but borrow mollusc shells, moving into larger homes as they grow. Sometimes one hermit crab will fight another hermit for its shell but will seldom attack a living snail. Rather, hermits usually occupy empty shells, trying out several until they find one that suits them. Hermit crab survival may depend on the number of empty shells available for them to use. Over twenty-five hermit crab species live in the northern Gulf.

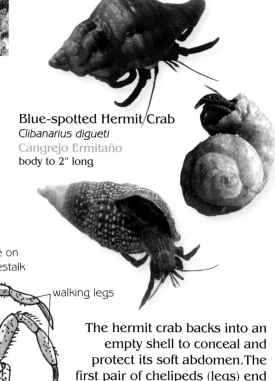

Blue-spotted Hermit Crab
Clibanarius digueti
Cangrejo Ermitaño
body to 2" long

Hermit crabs cluster in their borrowed shells.

Hermit crabs are omnivorous—they eat plant and animal material. Most active at night, they scavenge the reef.

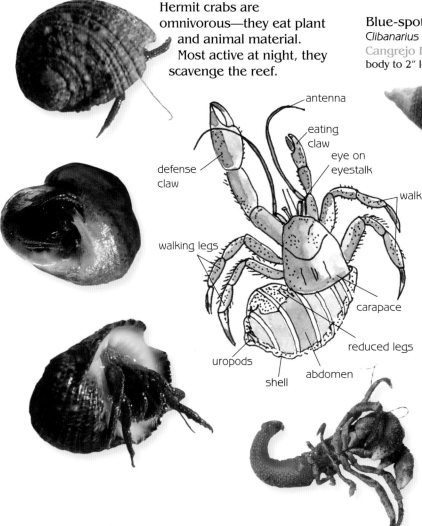

antenna

eating claw

eye on eyestalk

defense claw

walking legs

walking legs

carapace

reduced legs

uropods

abdomen

shell

The hermit crab backs into an empty shell to conceal and protect its soft abdomen. The first pair of chelipeds (legs) end in claws. The smaller right claw is used primarily for eating; the larger left claw is used for defense and blocks the shell opening when the crab retreats inside. The second and third pairs of legs are used for walking; the fourth and fifth pairs of legs hold the crab inside and help maneuver the shell. The uropods at the tip of the abdomen also grip the inside of the shell.

Regular Crabs  Arthropoda

Regular crabs live in rocky reef niches and crevices and under boulders. They are decapods (ten-legged) and use four pairs of legs for walking. Often disguised to match their habitat, they are difficult to see when immobile. The patient tidewalker will be rewarded by standing still and waiting for a crab to venture out.

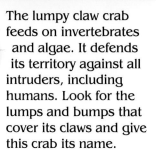

Lumpy Claw Crab
Eriphia squamata
Cangrejo
carapace 5" wide

The lumpy claw crab feeds on invertebrates and algae. It defends its territory against all intruders, including humans. Look for the lumps and bumps that cover its claws and give this crab its name.

cheliped (claw)

eye

Carapace differences distinguish males from females. This pair is mating, abdomen to abdomen, with the male on top.

walking legs

These crabs have four pairs of walking legs.

carapace (shell)

Hairy Crab
Pilumnus limosus
Cangrejo
carapace ½" wide

Look for sand outside a hole and then wait for the crab!

Crabs use various strategies to protect themselves. Some are aggressive in defending their territory, raising their claws to threaten and to attack. Others run away from danger, using speed and agility to escape. A few hide in plain sight by staying still and looking like part of the reef.

Hairy Crab
Pilumnus gonzalensis
Cangrejo
carapace ¾" wide

Decorator Crabs ～～～～～ Arthropoda

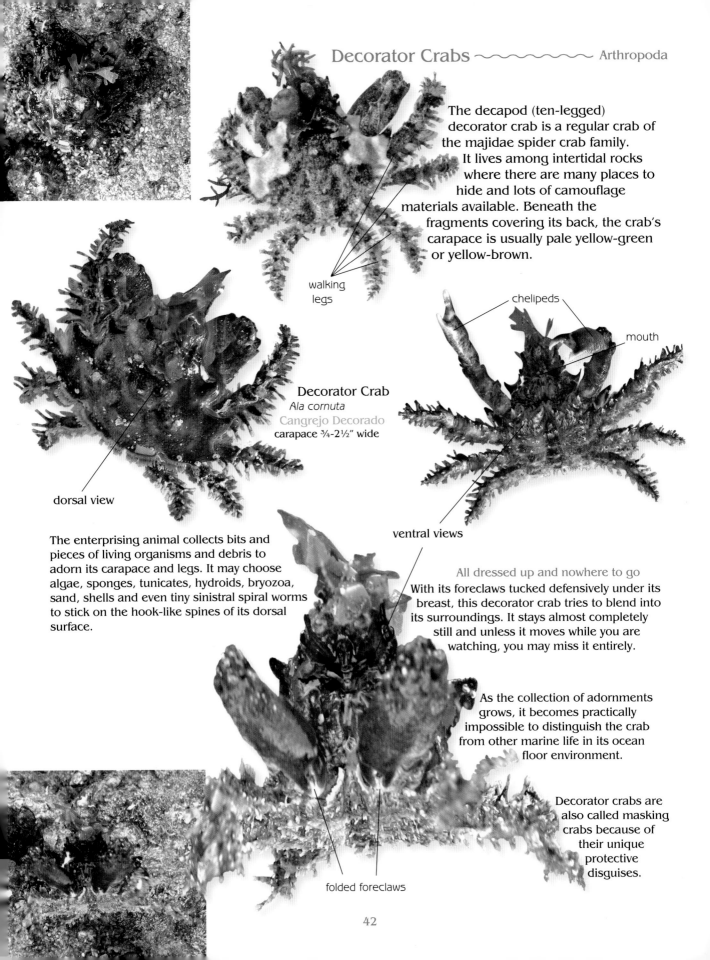

The decapod (ten-legged) decorator crab is a regular crab of the majidae spider crab family. It lives among intertidal rocks where there are many places to hide and lots of camouflage materials available. Beneath the fragments covering its back, the crab's carapace is usually pale yellow-green or yellow-brown.

walking legs

chelipeds

mouth

Decorator Crab
Ala cornuta
Cangrejo Decorado
carapace ¾-2½" wide

dorsal view

ventral views

The enterprising animal collects bits and pieces of living organisms and debris to adorn its carapace and legs. It may choose algae, sponges, tunicates, hydroids, bryozoa, sand, shells and even tiny sinistral spiral worms to stick on the hook-like spines of its dorsal surface.

All dressed up and nowhere to go
With its foreclaws tucked defensively under its breast, this decorator crab tries to blend into its surroundings. It stays almost completely still and unless it moves while you are watching, you may miss it entirely.

As the collection of adornments grows, it becomes practically impossible to distinguish the crab from other marine life in its ocean floor environment.

Decorator crabs are also called masking crabs because of their unique protective disguises.

folded foreclaws

42

Spider Crabs
~ Arthropoda

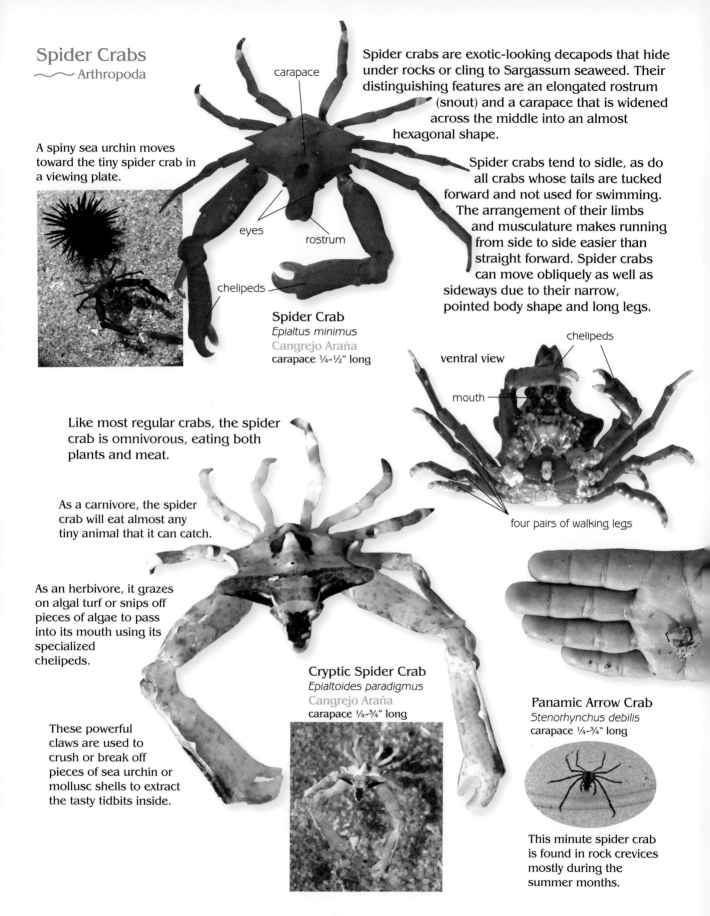

Spider crabs are exotic-looking decapods that hide under rocks or cling to Sargassum seaweed. Their distinguishing features are an elongated rostrum (snout) and a carapace that is widened across the middle into an almost hexagonal shape.

Spider crabs tend to sidle, as do all crabs whose tails are tucked forward and not used for swimming. The arrangement of their limbs and musculature makes running from side to side easier than straight forward. Spider crabs can move obliquely as well as sideways due to their narrow, pointed body shape and long legs.

A spiny sea urchin moves toward the tiny spider crab in a viewing plate.

carapace

eyes

rostrum

chelipeds

Spider Crab
Epialtus minimus
Cangrejo Araña
carapace ¼-½" long

ventral view

chelipeds

mouth

four pairs of walking legs

Like most regular crabs, the spider crab is omnivorous, eating both plants and meat.

As a carnivore, the spider crab will eat almost any tiny animal that it can catch.

As an herbivore, it grazes on algal turf or snips off pieces of algae to pass into its mouth using its specialized chelipeds.

These powerful claws are used to crush or break off pieces of sea urchin or mollusc shells to extract the tasty tidbits inside.

Cryptic Spider Crab
Epialtoides paradigmus
Cangrejo Araña
carapace ¼-¾" long

Panamic Arrow Crab
Stenorhynchus debilis
carapace ¼-¾" long

This minute spider crab is found in rock crevices mostly during the summer months.

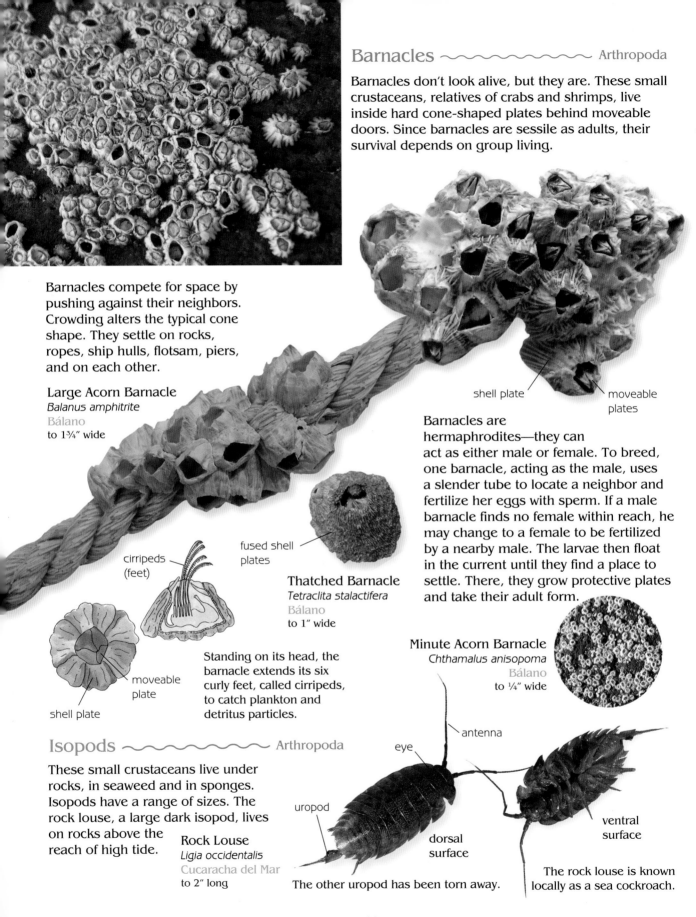

Barnacles ～～～～～～～ Arthropoda

Barnacles don't look alive, but they are. These small crustaceans, relatives of crabs and shrimps, live inside hard cone-shaped plates behind moveable doors. Since barnacles are sessile as adults, their survival depends on group living.

Barnacles compete for space by pushing against their neighbors. Crowding alters the typical cone shape. They settle on rocks, ropes, ship hulls, flotsam, piers, and on each other.

Large Acorn Barnacle
Balanus amphitrite
Bálano
to 1¾" wide

shell plate

moveable plates

Barnacles are hermaphrodites—they can act as either male or female. To breed, one barnacle, acting as the male, uses a slender tube to locate a neighbor and fertilize her eggs with sperm. If a male barnacle finds no female within reach, he may change to a female to be fertilized by a nearby male. The larvae then float in the current until they find a place to settle. There, they grow protective plates and take their adult form.

cirripeds (feet)

fused shell plates

Thatched Barnacle
Tetraclita stalactifera
Bálano
to 1" wide

moveable plate

shell plate

Standing on its head, the barnacle extends its six curly feet, called cirripeds, to catch plankton and detritus particles.

Minute Acorn Barnacle
Chthamalus anisopoma
Bálano
to ¼" wide

antenna

eye

Isopods ～～～～～～ Arthropoda

These small crustaceans live under rocks, in seaweed and in sponges. Isopods have a range of sizes. The rock louse, a large dark isopod, lives on rocks above the reach of high tide.

Rock Louse
Ligia occidentalis
Cucaracha del Mar
to 2" long

uropod

dorsal surface

ventral surface

The other uropod has been torn away.

The rock louse is known locally as a sea cockroach.

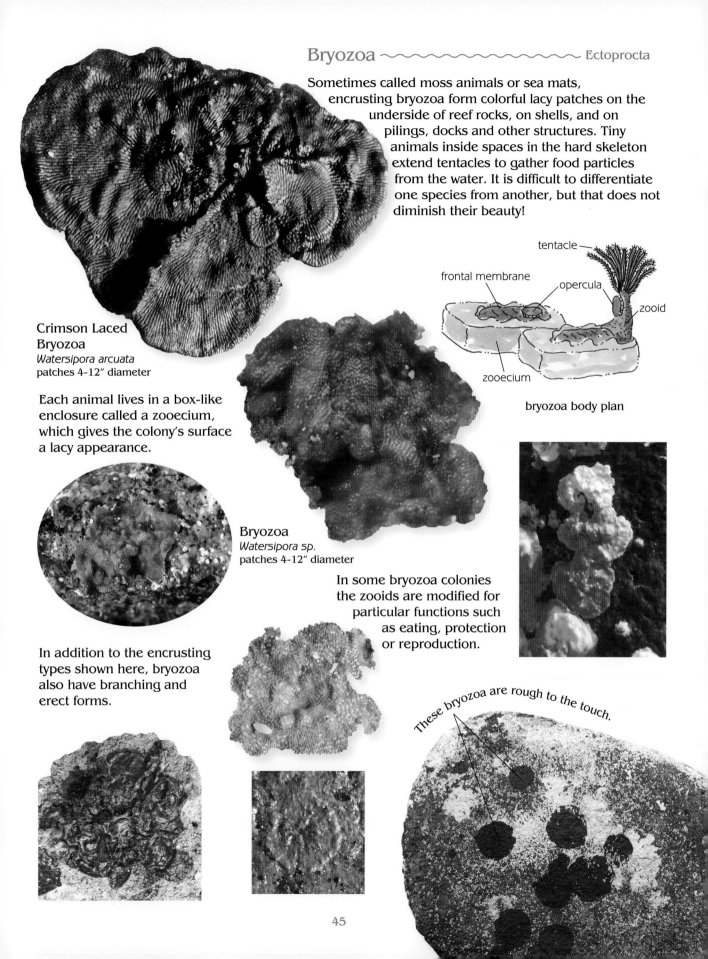

Bryozoa ～～～～～ Ectoprocta

Sometimes called moss animals or sea mats, encrusting bryozoa form colorful lacy patches on the underside of reef rocks, on shells, and on pilings, docks and other structures. Tiny animals inside spaces in the hard skeleton extend tentacles to gather food particles from the water. It is difficult to differentiate one species from another, but that does not diminish their beauty!

tentacle

frontal membrane

opercula

zooid

zooecium

bryozoa body plan

Crimson Laced Bryozoa
Watersipora arcuata
patches 4-12" diameter

Each animal lives in a box-like enclosure called a zooecium, which gives the colony's surface a lacy appearance.

Bryozoa
Watersipora sp.
patches 4-12" diameter

In some bryozoa colonies the zooids are modified for particular functions such as eating, protection or reproduction.

In addition to the encrusting types shown here, bryozoa also have branching and erect forms.

These bryozoa are rough to the touch.

Brittle Stars ~~~~~~ Echinodermata

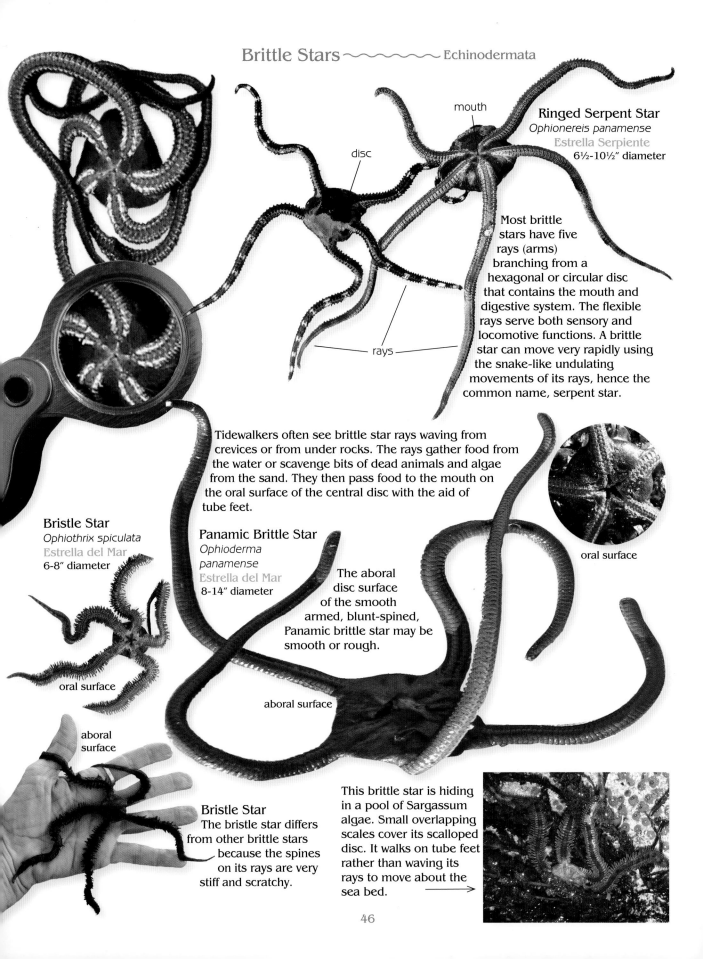

mouth

disc

Ringed Serpent Star
Ophionereis panamense
Estrella Serpiente
6½-10½" diameter

rays

Most brittle stars have five rays (arms) branching from a hexagonal or circular disc that contains the mouth and digestive system. The flexible rays serve both sensory and locomotive functions. A brittle star can move very rapidly using the snake-like undulating movements of its rays, hence the common name, serpent star.

Tidewalkers often see brittle star rays waving from crevices or from under rocks. The rays gather food from the water or scavenge bits of dead animals and algae from the sand. They then pass food to the mouth on the oral surface of the central disc with the aid of tube feet.

oral surface

Bristle Star
Ophiothrix spiculata
Estrella del Mar
6-8" diameter

Panamic Brittle Star
Ophioderma panamense
Estrella del Mar
8-14" diameter

The aboral disc surface of the smooth armed, blunt-spined, Panamic brittle star may be smooth or rough.

oral surface

aboral surface

aboral surface

Bristle Star
The bristle star differs from other brittle stars because the spines on its rays are very stiff and scratchy.

This brittle star is hiding in a pool of Sargassum algae. Small overlapping scales cover its scalloped disc. It walks on tube feet rather than waving its rays to move about the sea bed. →

46

Basket stars are brittle stars whose five rays subdivide and curl up into successively more complex branches until they intertwine to form a basket-like shape. They rarely appear in the intertidal zone but may occasionally be washed ashore by extreme tides or brought up from deep water in fishing nets.

Basket Star   dorsal view
Astrocaneum spinosum
Estrella Canastilia
5-10" diameter

         ventral view

Alexander's Spiny Brittle Star
Ophiocoma alexandri
Estrella del mar
3-12½" diameter

Long glass-like spines adorn the rays of this unusual brittle star, giving the rays a fuzzy, even hairy look. Its central disc has a very rough texture because uneven granules cover its aboral surface.

Brittle stars are brittle because the calcareous plates that cover their rays are held together by relatively soft, fragile tissue. Rays can easily break accidentally or be torn off by predators.

Black Spiny Brittle Star
Ophiocoma aethiops
Estrella del Mar
3½-17½" diameter

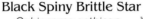

aboral surface

oral surface

central disc

A frightened brittle star may use a spontaneous defense mechanism called autotomy (self-cut) to cast off or sever part of an arm that is trapped. The remaining section of ray will later regenerate.

Banded Brittle Star
Ophionereis annulata
Estrella del Mar
3-12½" diameter

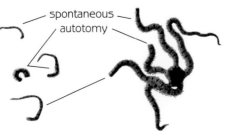

spontaneous
autotomy

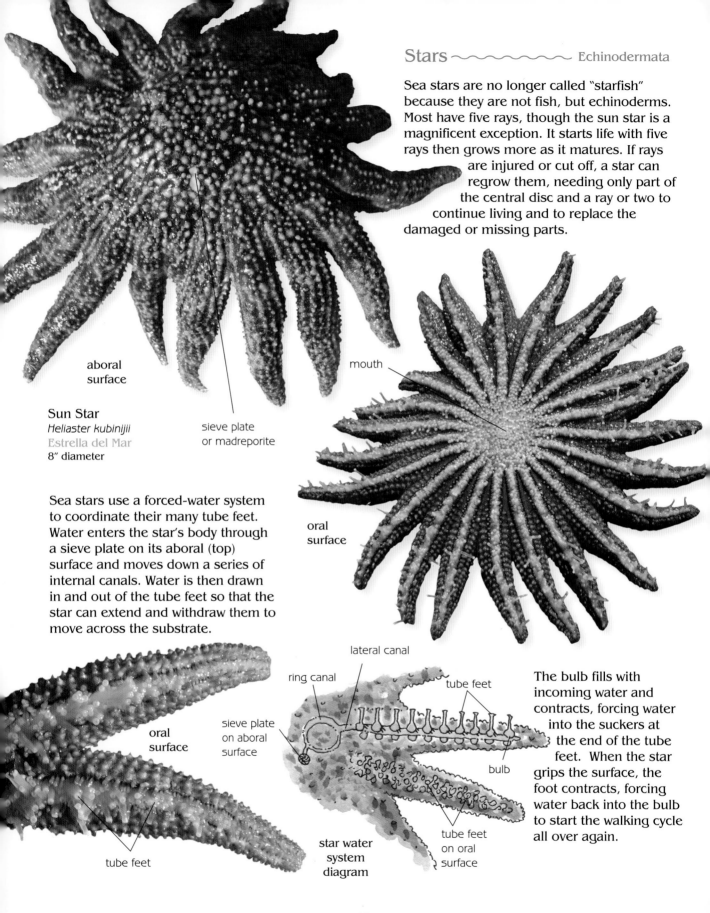

Sea stars are no longer called "starfish" because they are not fish, but echinoderms. Most have five rays, though the sun star is a magnificent exception. It starts life with five rays then grows more as it matures. If rays are injured or cut off, a star can regrow them, needing only part of the central disc and a ray or two to continue living and to replace the damaged or missing parts.

aboral
surface

mouth

Sun Star
Heliaster kubinijii
Estrella del Mar
8" diameter

sieve plate
or madreporite

oral
surface

Sea stars use a forced-water system to coordinate their many tube feet. Water enters the star's body through a sieve plate on its aboral (top) surface and moves down a series of internal canals. Water is then drawn in and out of the tube feet so that the star can extend and withdraw them to move across the substrate.

lateral canal

ring canal

tube feet

oral
surface

sieve plate
on aboral
surface

bulb

tube feet

The bulb fills with incoming water and contracts, forcing water into the suckers at the end of the tube feet. When the star grips the surface, the foot contracts, forcing water back into the bulb to start the walking cycle all over again.

star water
system
diagram

tube feet
on oral
surface

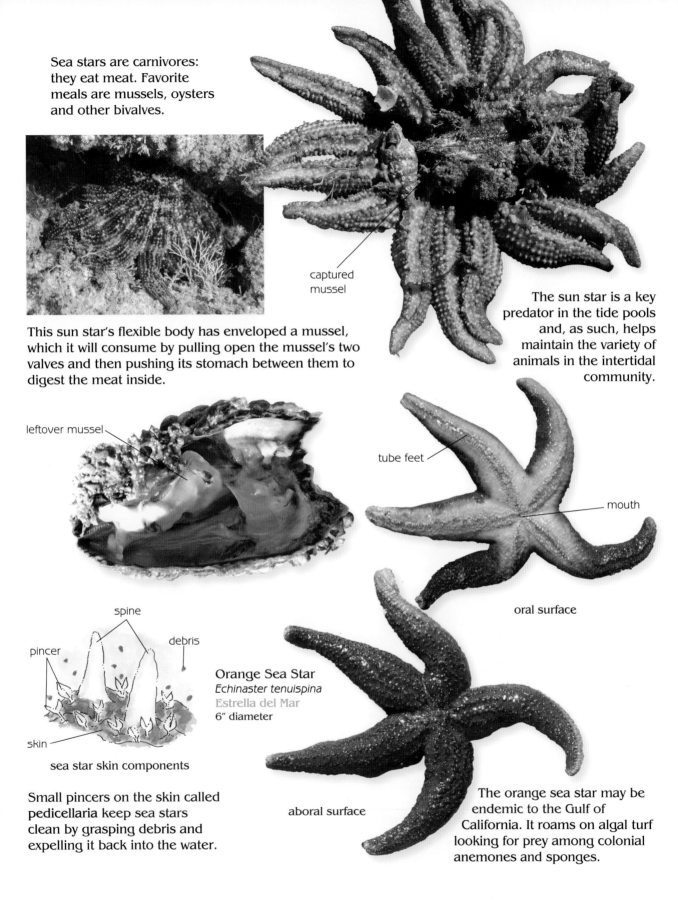

Sea stars are carnivores: they eat meat. Favorite meals are mussels, oysters and other bivalves.

captured mussel

This sun star's flexible body has enveloped a mussel, which it will consume by pulling open the mussel's two valves and then pushing its stomach between them to digest the meat inside.

The sun star is a key predator in the tide pools and, as such, helps maintain the variety of animals in the intertidal community.

leftover mussel

tube feet

mouth

oral surface

spine

debris

pincer

skin

sea star skin components

Orange Sea Star
Echinaster tenuispina
Estrella del Mar
6" diameter

aboral surface

Small pincers on the skin called pedicellaria keep sea stars clean by grasping debris and expelling it back into the water.

The orange sea star may be endemic to the Gulf of California. It roams on algal turf looking for prey among colonial anemones and sponges.

Spiny Sea Urchins ～～～ Echinodermata

Most spiny urchins live in the safety of small crevices or are attached to the undersides of rocks where they won't be dislodged by ocean waves or currents. An urchin's calcareous test (skeleton) consists of many small plates that fit together to form a rigid case. The plates bear small knobs that serve as ball and socket joints controlling the movement of the sharp spines (tubercles) covering the urchin.

The tube feet of a spiny sea urchin protrude through five radiating ambulacral grooves (channels). These form a distinct star pattern on both oral and aboral surfaces.

urchin test
top view

urchin test
bottom view

Purple Sea Urchin
Echinometra vanbrunti
Erizo
test 1½" diameter
spines to 2½" long

Black Sea Urchin
Arbacia incisa
Erizo
test 1½" diameter
spines to 2½" long

Juvenile black urchins are initially red, turning purple and finally black as they mature.

spines

tube feet

pedicellaria

Aristotle's lantern

Numerous double rows of tube feet help the urchin to move over the reef in stilt-like locomotion and to cling to rocks. Specialized pedicellaria (flexible pincers) are interspersed among the urchin's spines for cleaning or grasping detrital materials to be used as camouflage. Some pedicellaria are poisonous for protection against predators like crabs, stars, rays and gulls.

Aristotle's lantern is the spiny urchin's feeding apparatus. It consists of five sharp teeth and supporting musculature. It is used to bite or scrape algae off the substrate.

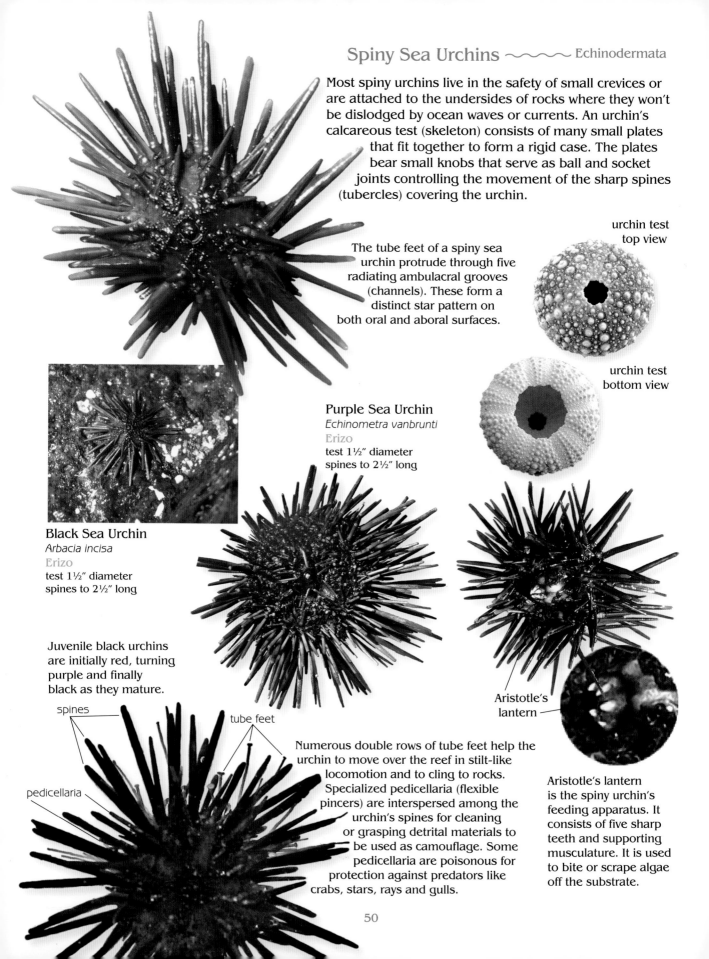

50

Slate Pencil Urchins 〜〜〜 Echinodermata

The slate pencil urchin is a rock borer and takes refuge in small cavities in the reef to protect itself from its enemies, mainly sea stars and triggerfish. It is a vegetarian browser that traps bits of algae in its spines and passes them around to its mouth. It also scrapes encrusting organisms off rocks and bites them into small bits with its five sharp teeth.

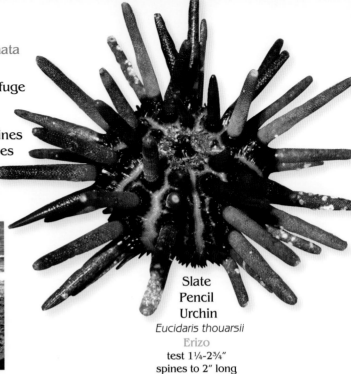

Slate
Pencil
Urchin
Eucidaris thouarsii
Erizo
test 1¼-2¾"
spines to 2" long

During the writing of this book, the authors photographed the same urchin under the same rock ledge over a three-year span. The ledge was exposed only at extreme low tides, but the urchin was there each time we were able to reach the site.

A slate pencil urchin's age may be determined by rings of pigment deposited on the outer plates of its spines at the end of each summer's growth period. Some are known to live at least eight years. This photo of a Pacific urchin's test shows growth rings and the connective spinal ball joints that facilitate locomotion. ⟶

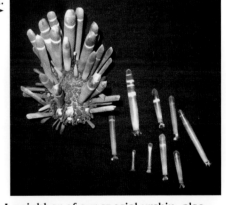

This particular urchin seems able to move freely in and out of its chosen burrow in search of food and then return to the safety of its den.

A neighbor of our special urchin, also a permanent resident, was beset with numerous sponges growing in its burrow and encircling some of its spines.

This urchin appears to be wedged between two large rocks. Even its ability to rotate its spines in many directions may not allow it enough wiggle room to free itself.

51

Sea Cucumbers ～～～～ Echinodermata

Giant Cortez Cucumber
Isostichopus fuscus
Pepino del Mar
10" long

Sea cucumbers are echinoderms whose spines are beneath the skin. They have no rays but do have the typical five-part symmetry of other echinoderms. Five rows of tube feet are used for crawling and for moving food to the mouth. The mouth is surrounded by branching tentacles that also gather food. Their bodies feel leathery and contract when they are out of the water.

warty skeletal bumps

dorsal surface

Cucumbers live under ledges and rocks. When threatened by starfish, crabs or people, they may eject strings of sticky mucus to give them time to escape. Sea cucumbers can eviserate, that is, expel their internal organs, a tactic thought to occupy predators, allowing the body wall to escape and to later regrow the missing organs.

ventral surface

rows of tube feet

Spotted Cucumber
Holothuria impatiens
Pepino del Mar
to 6" long

Also called bêche de mer, the sea cucumber is consumed as a delicacy in China where it is thought to have aphrodisiac properties.

branching tentacles

sea cucumber body plan

tube feet

Sulphur Cucumber
Holothuria lubrica
Pepino del Mar
to 6" long

Tunicates ~~~~~~~~~~~~~~~~ Chordata

Colonial tunicates live in flexible sacks called tunics that protect the soft bodies within. Because they can forcibly eject water, tunicates are called sea squirts. They make colorful patches on intertidal surfaces. Scientists examine tunicate anatomy to identify species.

Colonial Tunicates
Ascidia spp.
colony size dependent on species and habitat
Tunicados

The gel-like matrix in which tunicates live may be semi-transparent. It is slick to the touch. In contrast, bryozoa are rough and sponges are resiliant.

This solitary tunicate is called a sea grape.

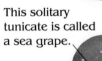

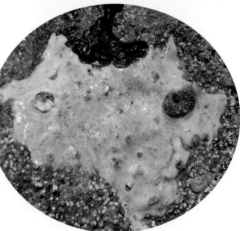

Colonial Tunicates

solitary tunicate

Lancelets ~~~~~~~~~~~~~~~~ Chordata

Lancelet, Amphioxus
Branchiostoma californiense
to 3" long

Lancelets and tunicate tadpoles have nerve cords in the back, similar to those of vertebrates; thus tunicates and lancelets are placed in the chordata phylum.

The lancelet has no brain and no eyes.

oral cirri

These worm-like creatures live in sand. Once exposed, they writhe, squirm and burrow quickly. Sting rays eat lancelets.

The Omnivores

Size is an important factor in predation. Bigger creatures eat smaller ones, and larger species have a much wider variety of choices. Omnivores include both carnivores and herbivores.

The carnivorous swimming crab likes snails and fish.

Crabs are an omnivorous group. Most crabs are carnivorous critters that eat any kind of meat they can catch with their claws. However, many shore crabs are herbivores that feed on bits of algal turf using specialized spoon-shaped chelipeds.

Omnivorous encrusting sponges feed on microscopic bits of bacteria, algae and detritus filtered through their sea water exchange systems.

Nudibranchs and sea slugs are omnivores, too. Herbivorous nudibranchs use their radulae to scrape algae off rocks. Carnivorous aeolids use nematocysts to stun larger prey like anemones, hydroids and sponges.

Gastropod snails constitute another main category of omnivores. Most are carnivorous, and use their radulae as "meat hooks" to snare their food. Cones spear molluscs and fish with their harpoon-like, single-tooth radulae and cowries eat sea squirts and other gastropods. Moon snails like clams; drills prey on both clams and oysters.

Stars are another omnivorous group. Heliasters eat mussels, oysters and sea cucumbers, using digestive enzymes to dissolve their prey. Sand stars are partial to urchins, scallops and other bivalves, while brittle stars scavenge for dead animals and detritus on the sea floor.

Tops, turbans and nerites are herbivorous snails.

The Carnivores

It's usually a case of "eat or be eaten" in the world of carnivores. They are true predators and they eat only meat, dead or alive.

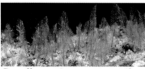

Small crustaceans are the main diet of hydroids.

Barnacles filter plankton and detritus from sea water drifting past their colonies.

Anemones can trap small bivalves, crabs, shrimp and even fish in their stinging tentacles.

Sand dollars filter-feed on diatoms, plankton and barnacle larva.

Mussel eggs, small molluscs and crustaceans are favorites of flatworms, while ribbon worms eat molluscs, small fish and other worms.

The Herbivores

Herbivores are not predators; they are preyed upon. They include bivalves, urchins, sea hares and some sea slugs.

Irritating isopods may seem to be carnivores that prey upon humans; but don't worry, they are strictly herbivorous and eat seaweeds!

Textures, Tracks and Trails

Patterns and textures of the shore can be a source of wonderment for tidewalkers and photographers.

beach shingle

sand ripples

coquina ridges

ripples with ridges

Ripples and Rills

Sand ripples are caused by water or wind or both. They usually run parallel to the waterline. Rill patterns are formed as little streams of water drain perpendicular to the shore when the tide recedes. Broken ripples result when the water rills cut through the sand ripples.

water rills with ripples

sand ripples

broken ripples cut by rills

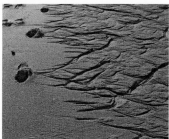
sand rills

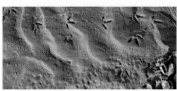

Ripples add new dimensions to reflections in the water.

Telltale Tracks and Trails

Shore birds leave tracks in the sand as they search for food.

Some invertebrates can be identified by their tracks on the surface.

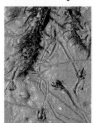
cerith trails

olive track

clam track

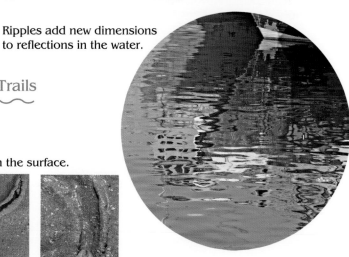

55

Tidepool Fish
~ Chordata

Sonora Blenny
Malacoctenus gigas
Trambollo
to 3" long

Spotted Sand Bass
Paralabrax maculatofasciatus
Cabrilla de Roca
this juvenile 2" long
adults to 22"

Schools of little fish dart about in the tide pools. Some are the juveniles of larger fish that swim in deeper water. Others are intertidal residents, staying in the tide pools when the water recedes. Reflections off the surface make identification difficult. Try a small net for a closer look, and then return the fish quickly to its home.

Panamic Sergeant Major
Abudefduf troschelii
Banderita, Pintano, Chopa
to 10" long

Sonora Clingfish
Tomicodon humeralis
Chupapiedra
to 3" long
dorsal surface

ventral surface
(through glass)

sucker
disk

Schools of juvenile sergeant majors swim in the tide pools.

Clingfish thrive in mid and high intertidal zones, using mucus secretions to avoid drying. They can be found attached by a sucker disk to the underside of rocks, in tidepool niches and, like the one below, in shell fragments.

Slender gobies, some bright, others cryptically colored, can be seen in sandy-bottom rocky-shore tide pools and muddy esteros.

Longtail Goby
Gobionellus sagittula
Góbio
to 4½" long

You can put a clingfish gently in a glass dish to see how the sucker disk works.

Tadpole Clingfish
Gobiesox pinniger
Chupapiedra
to 3½" long

Shore Birds ∿∿∿∿∿ Chordata

The waters of the Sea of Cortez are rich hunting grounds for shore birds. Salt marshes and esteros provide safe havens for breeding pairs.

A pelican and a cormorant guard a local fishing boat pier.

A pelican squadron follows the shoreline in fish-spotting formation, each bird flying in rhythmic sequence.

Fledgling ospreys eagerly await the return of the parent birds that bring bits of regurgitated fish from the shore.

Osprey

↑ A gull watches for leftovers as pelicans ↓ dive for fish in a feeding frenzy. Splash!

A great blue heron wades near the rocky shore looking for fish. Herons and egrets are often seen hunting for food ↓ in the early morning or evening light.

A flock of migrating American avocets pause in an estero to rest and feed at ↓ morning low tide.

Sea gulls, the scavengers of the shore, will eat almost any kind of flesh, dead or alive. Gulls are important in keeping the beach clean.

At the Sandy and Muddy Shore

Tricky Tides on Sandy Shores

Twice daily, sea water alternately fills, then drains Cholla Bay and similar bays in the northern Gulf. High and low tides transform the bay from a broad expanse of deep water into a shallow wonderland for beachcombers and tidewalkers.

Where does the water go?

Fluctuations in the gravitational pull of the moon, sun and earth, in relation to each other, cause fluctuations in water levels that produce tidal flows. Therefore, the sea level in general rises and falls as tidal waves pass through it. The water doesn't actually go anywhere except toward and away from the shore line.

High tide

Low tide

In contrast to the immense progressive tides of the open oceans of the world, standing-wave tides in the long, narrow Gulf of California slosh back and forth rather like water in a bathtub.

Look for tidal surge channels flowing toward the open sea like rivers in the sand. Tidewalkers often see mobile creatures such as scallops, octopuses, crabs and sand dollars searching for food in surge channels.

Slack water periods occur about an hour after each high tide and low tide when the sea level is not rising or falling. The best time to study intertidal sea life is at low water slack, the hour before the sea level begins to rise again.

Shoreline distances can be deceiving, so look for signs of change and head for shore well in advance of incoming tides. Turning tides may sometimes leave unwary clamdiggers, tidewalkers or their vehicles stranded.

High tide

Low tide

Salt marshes form where rivers meet the sea, depositing sand, silt and mud at the junctures. Changing tides affect water depth, temperature and salinity, resulting in super-rich habitats and breeding grounds for shoreline creatures, fish, birds and plants. Coastal wetlands are known as the nurseries of the sea.

Tidewalking on Sandy Shores

Sandy shores provide little surface shelter for seashore creatures. Most sea life will either follow the water as it recedes or burrow deeply into still-moist sand below to await the returning tide. There they will eat the tiny organisms between the sand grains. Although sandy beaches may look and feel soft, they are actually made of shell and rock pieces, pulverized by tumbling in the waves and rubbing against one another.

Look in, on or under the sand

anemones   anemone   sand star   egg cases   sandworm   murex   spider crab   featherduster   sand dollar

Tidewalkers will find fascinating combinations of symbiotic creatures in the water or on open sand along the beach. Certain signs on the surface indicate what animals may be below.

 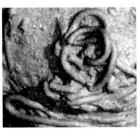

A growing pile of sand is a sure sign there's a lug worm at work beneath the surface.

A vast sandy beach can be literally covered with hundreds of thousands of tiny holes, each inhabited by a ghost shrimp, fiddler crab or other burrowing critter.

Periwinkles and oyster drills find empty pen shells ideal places to deposit their egg strings. If you gently turn over a pen shell, you may find these critters at work.

If you come across an obvious star shape and scoop away the surrounding sand, you may find a sea star hiding below. Be sure to cover it up again when you have finished observing it.

An octopus may construct an elaborate den using shells and rocks. It will also take refuge in an empty bivalve, bottle or soda can if it needs shelter in an emergency.

Burrowing Sand Anemone
Cnidaria

First seen as a small round depression, this burrowing anemone can dig itself deep into the sand when disturbed. Its rough worm-like body tapers downward under the sand and swells into a bulbous anchor to prevent its being pulled out by a hungry bird or curious tidewalker. Getting a closer look at its warty base requires rapid digging to catch it before it disappears.

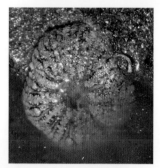

Like cnidarians of the rocky shore, the burrowing sand anemone folds its nematocyst-bearing tentacles into its gut when it is exposed to the air at low tide and re-opens them when the water returns.

Exercise care when digging after a critter under the sand to avoid injuring the animal. Be sure to return it to its original location after you examine or photograph it.

Collared Anemone
Phyllactis sp.
Anémona
collar 1-2" diameter

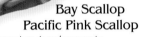

Scallops ～～～～～～～～～ Mollusca

Since ancient times scallops have been prized for food and have served as symbols of sea life in decorative arts the world over.

Two main types of scallops, bay scallops and Pacific calico scallops, are common in the Sea of Cortez. Tidewalkers see both types of shells on the beach, but usually find live specimens only in deeper water at low tide.

Bay Scallop
Pacific Pink Scallop
Leptopecten tumbezensis
Bivalvo Pechina
1-3" wide

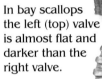

In bay scallops the left (top) valve is almost flat and darker than the right valve.

top valve exterior

bottom valve exterior

The right (bottom) valve is larger and more convex than the left. This allows the two halves to fit tightly together, to form a strong seal against predators.

top valve interior

bottom valve interior

Sea stars prey on bivalves including scallops.

The top and bottom valves of the calico scallop are both convex and almost mirror images of each other, with a wide variety of mottled patterns. Colors range from pure white to yellow, orange, brown, purple or black. When the hinge is open, the edge of the mantle is visible around the scalloped edge. The mantle has rows of tentacles and ocelli (eye-like sensors) that can detect light, shadows and motion.

Pacific Calico Scallop
Argopecten circularis
Almeja Voladora
Escalopa
1-3½" long

The scallop is a motile (free-moving) creature, unattached to any substrate. It evades its enemies using water jets to propel itself out of danger. The leading edge (hinge) contains the abductor muscle (the edible part of the scallop). The abductor muscle alternately opens and closes the valves in a rapid clapping motion that expels water jets out of the rear (scalloped) edge. The result is a jerky zig-zag style of swimming rapidly away from an attacker.

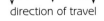

water jets

direction of travel

Strandline Shells
~~~ Mollusca

At low tide most clams and snails burrow out of sight in the sand and mud. The empty shells scattered on the beach are clues to the species that hide below.

radial ribs

concentric ribs

Clam
Chione sp.
Almeja China
3" wide

Venus Clam
Chione sp.
Almeja Piedra
2" wide

lattice

radial

concentric

shell rib design

Horn Shell
Cerithidea mazatlanica
Caracolillo, Ceritídeo
1" long

Tower Shell
Turritella sp.
Torrecilla
5" long

radial ribs

Tellin
Tellina sp.
Almeja Telina
1" wide

The colorful tellin is used to make shell-craft flowers.

thick ridges

Venus Clam
Chione tumens
Almeja
2" wide

White Cockle
Trachycardium panamense
Berberecho
4" wide

Bittersweet Clam
Glycymeris gigantea
Almendra del Mar
5" wide

The bittersweet clam gets its name from its taste.

Venus Clam
Dosinia dunkeri
Almeja Reina
5" wide

Clams and Cockles ～～～～～～～ Mollusca

Clam and cockle valves are held together by a powerful hinge ligament. The clam inside contracts and relaxes its muscle to open and close its shell. The shell grows as the mantle deposits shell material on the outer edges.

Chocolate Clam
Megapitaria squalida
Almeja Chocolate
to 1½" wide

To hide, the clam extends its foot into the sand or mud where the foot swells to form an anchor. This allows the mollusc to pull itself below the surface. The foot then deflates and extends again to go deeper, taking the clam out of danger.

valves

foot

siphons

To filter microscopic plankton from sea water, the clam uses one siphon to suck nutrients in and another to expel wastes.

You may find clams by looking for bumps and slashes in the sand, called "show" by clamdiggers. Sometimes the clam shell will be exposed on the surface.

tube worms

Basket Cockle
Clinocardium nuttalli
Berberecho
to 3" wide

The basket cockle shows distinct growth increments. The rough periostracum shields the exterior from damage.

foot

Giant Panamic Cockle
Laevicardium elatum
Almeja Amarilla Gigante
to 6" wide

Large cockles are still collected as a food source. These shells have been found in ancient and historical middens along the Gulf coast and in Arizona. Discoveries include etched valves and pieces made into ornaments and bracelets.

Giant Panamic Cockle
Laevicardium elatum
Almeja Amarilla Gigante
to 6" wide

A carnivorous drill works on a clam dinner.

Drill
Eupleura muriciformes
Caracol
to 2" long

Live and empty bivalve shells of every size provide handy homes and lunch boxes for a variety of intertidal dwellers.

Spiny Cup and Saucer Limpet
Crucibulum spinosum
Lapa Espinosa
to ½" wide

Clam
Chione sp.
Almeja China
to 3" wide

California Chione
Chione californienses
Almeja
to 1½" wide

This spiny cup and saucer limpet makes its home on a clam.

Spotted Cerith
Cerithium stercusmuscarum
Caracolillo Ceritídeo
to 2" long

Atypical of bivalves, this scallop's two valves are not alike.

rounded

flat

Scallop
Pecten sp.
Almeja Voladora
to 3" wide

Ceriths nibble on an open chocolate clam.

Pen Shells 〜〜〜 Mollusca

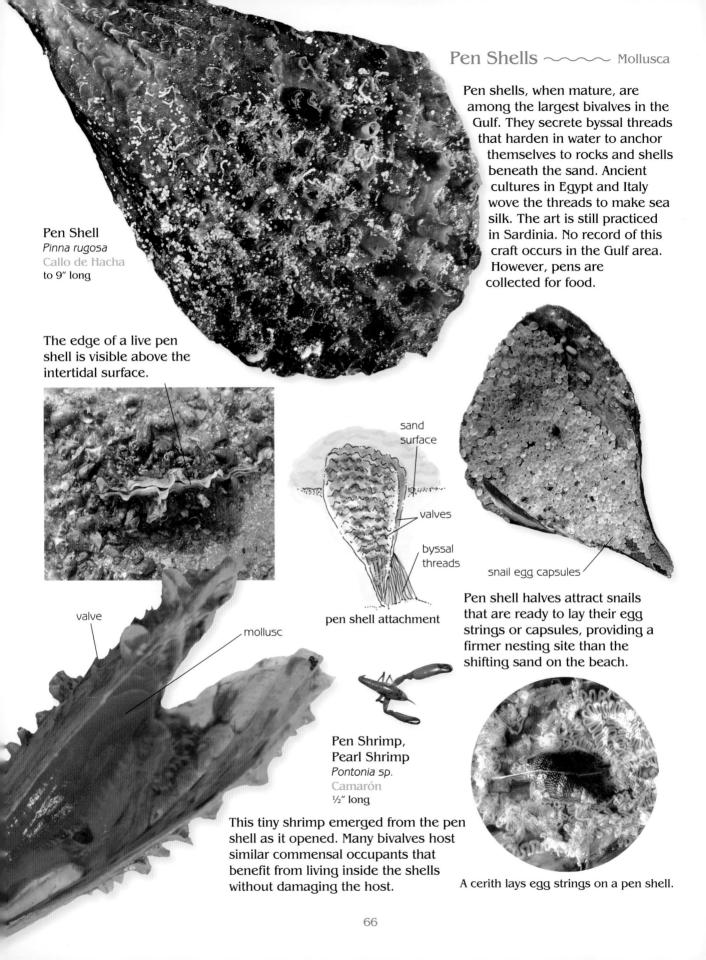

Pen Shell
Pinna rugosa
Callo de Hacha
to 9" long

Pen shells, when mature, are among the largest bivalves in the Gulf. They secrete byssal threads that harden in water to anchor themselves to rocks and shells beneath the sand. Ancient cultures in Egypt and Italy wove the threads to make sea silk. The art is still practiced in Sardinia. No record of this craft occurs in the Gulf area. However, pens are collected for food.

The edge of a live pen shell is visible above the intertidal surface.

sand surface

valves

byssal threads

pen shell attachment

snail egg capsules

Pen shell halves attract snails that are ready to lay their egg strings or capsules, providing a firmer nesting site than the shifting sand on the beach.

valve

mollusc

Pen Shrimp, Pearl Shrimp
Pontonia sp.
Camarón
½" long

This tiny shrimp emerged from the pen shell as it opened. Many bivalves host similar commensal occupants that benefit from living inside the shells without damaging the host.

A cerith lays egg strings on a pen shell.

Egg Capsules ～～～ Mollusca

Many snails lay their eggs in capsules clustered on rocks, on other shells or on each other. Each species has its own unique way of reproducing. In springtime it seems as if the shore is blooming. When you see eggs, look nearby—the depositing snail may still be present.

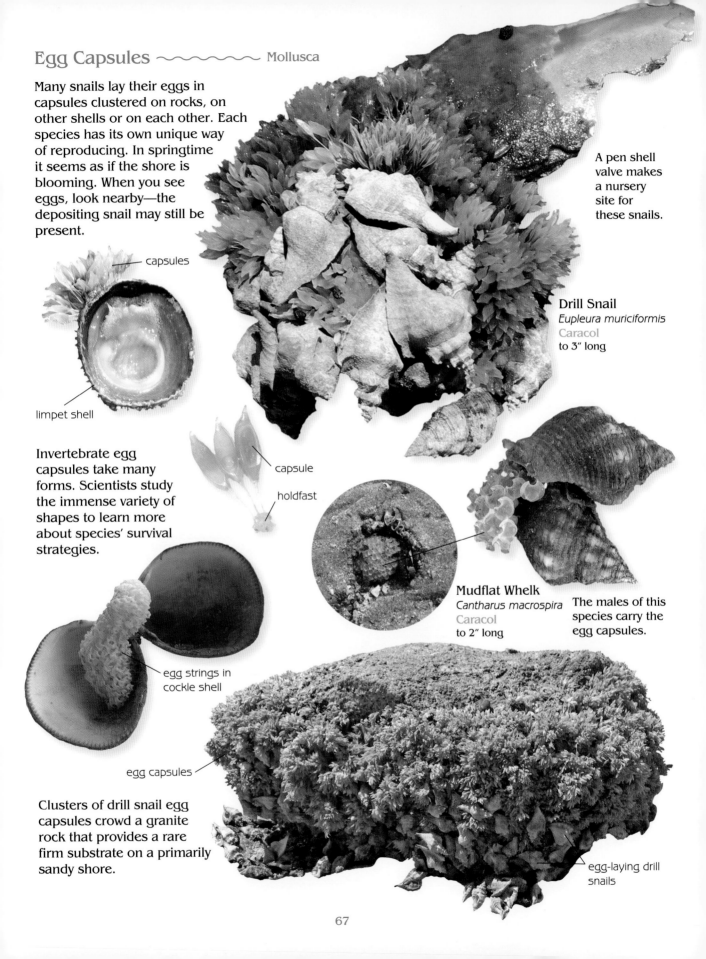

capsules

limpet shell

A pen shell valve makes a nursery site for these snails.

Drill Snail
Eupleura muriciformis
Caracol
to 3" long

Invertebrate egg capsules take many forms. Scientists study the immense variety of shapes to learn more about species' survival strategies.

capsule

holdfast

Mudflat Whelk
Cantharus macrospira
Caracol
to 2" long

The males of this species carry the egg capsules.

egg strings in cockle shell

egg capsules

Clusters of drill snail egg capsules crowd a granite rock that provides a rare firm substrate on a primarily sandy shore.

egg-laying drill snails

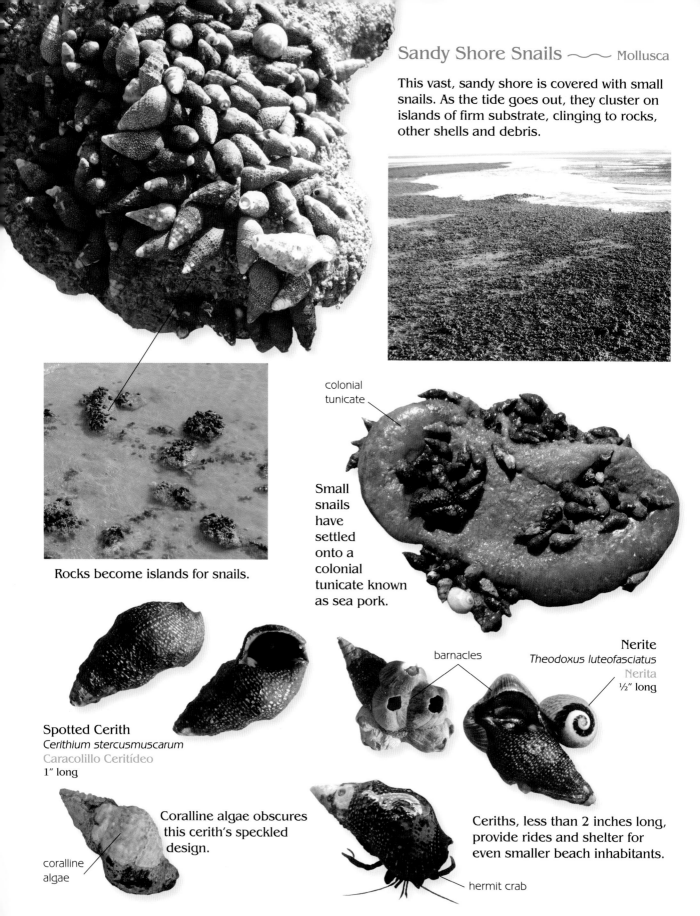

Sandy Shore Snails ~ Mollusca

This vast, sandy shore is covered with small snails. As the tide goes out, they cluster on islands of firm substrate, clinging to rocks, other shells and debris.

Rocks become islands for snails.

colonial tunicate

Small snails have settled onto a colonial tunicate known as sea pork.

Spotted Cerith
Cerithium stercusmuscarum
Caracolillo Ceritídeo
1" long

Coralline algae obscures this cerith's speckled design.

coralline algae

barnacles

Nerite
Theodoxus luteofasciatus
Nerita
½" long

hermit crab

Ceriths, less than 2 inches long, provide rides and shelter for even smaller beach inhabitants.

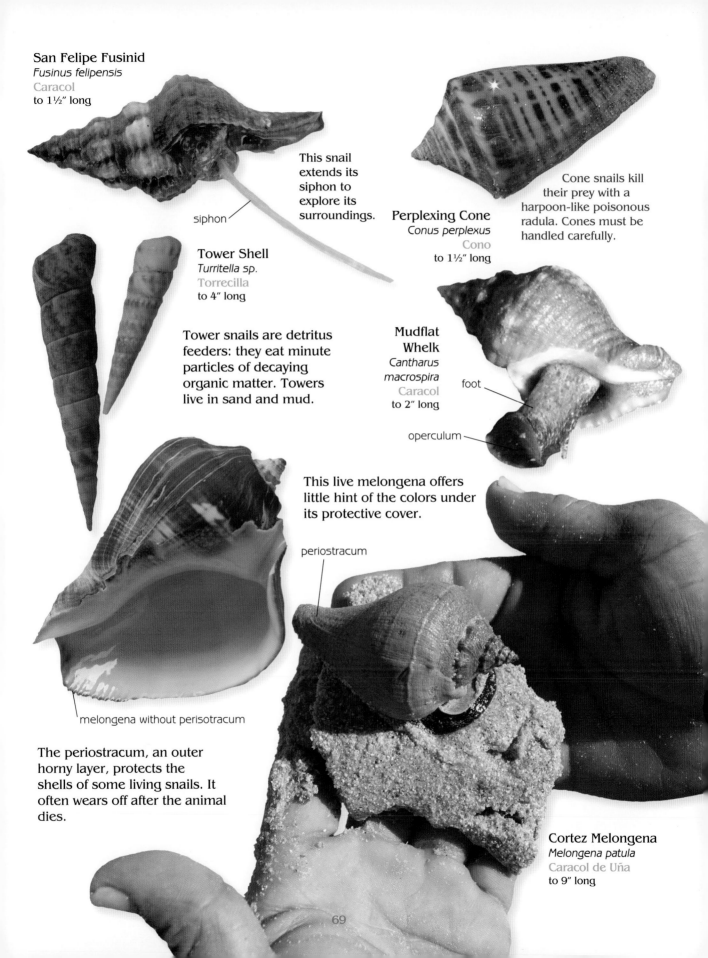

San Felipe Fusinid
Fusinus felipensis
Caracol
to 1½" long

This snail extends its siphon to explore its surroundings.

siphon

Perplexing Cone
Conus perplexus
Cono
to 1½" long

Cone snails kill their prey with a harpoon-like poisonous radula. Cones must be handled carefully.

Tower Shell
Turritella sp.
Torrecilla
to 4" long

Tower snails are detritus feeders: they eat minute particles of decaying organic matter. Towers live in sand and mud.

Mudflat Whelk
Cantharus macrospira
Caracol
to 2" long

foot

operculum

This live melongena offers little hint of the colors under its protective cover.

periostracum

melongena without perisotracum

The periostracum, an outer horny layer, protects the shells of some living snails. It often wears off after the animal dies.

Cortez Melongena
Melongena patula
Caracol de Uña
to 9" long

Moon Snails ～～ Mollusca

Moon snails prowl the sandy surface in search of clams and other prey. The moons then engulf the meal with their large feet. Moons are sometimes called shark's eyes or cat's eyes. Look for them and their unusual egg collars in the spring and summer on sandy beaches.

Polished Moon Snail
Natica chemnitzii
Caracol de Luna
1" diameter

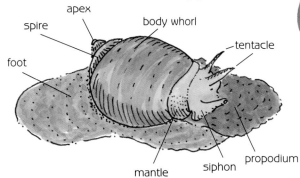

moon snail body plan

apex
spire
body whorl
foot
tentacle
mantle
siphon
propodium

body whorl

Moon Snail
Polinices sp.
Caracol de Luna
1" diameter

operculum

Moon snails use their radulae to drill holes and suck out the contents of prey they capture. As moons travel on the surface or just beneath it, they leave characteristic trails.

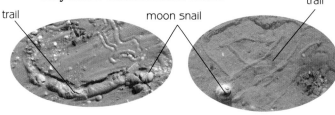

trail
moon snail
trail

moon snail eggs in a matrix of sand and mucus

A moon snail leaves its egg collar. The collar will slowly disintegrate and release the larval moons.

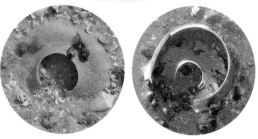

moon collars in the sand

Pygmy Octopus ～～～～～ Mollusca

The pygmy octopus is common to sandy or muddy shores and is frequently found in empty bivalves, snail shells or discarded containers like bottles. Normally a pale translucent pinkish-tan, it can change color to fit its situation and location.

Its amazing brain has decentralized satellites located in each of its eight arms, so each arm can act independently of the others.

ventral view seen through a glass plate

Pygmy Octopus
Octopus digueti
Pulpito
total width 8-10" across

dorsal view

How can a clam shell with a pygmy octopus inside be distinguished from a live clam?
• It doesn't immediately disappear into deeper sand.
• It weighs less than a live clam of equal size.
• When a shell is occupied by a pygmy octopus, it is possible to pull the halves apart with your fingertips.
• It would take a knife or sharp blade to pry open a live clam.

A lucky tidewalker may find a pygmy octopus in a tightly closed clam shell on top of the sand.

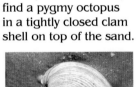

An octopus bite can be painful, so keep your fingers away from its sharp beak!

When exposed in a clam shell, a frightened pygmy octopus keeps trying to pull the halves of the shell back together, no matter how many times it must begin again.

This mysterious burrow construction was found at low tide in the middle of a shallow expanse of sandy shore in the upper Gulf. One can speculate that it is probably the work of a master marine architect, an octopus.

Sandy Shore Crabs
Arthropoda

A variety of crabs live in the mud and sand of esteros and tidal flats. The most noticeable are the swimming crabs, masking crabs and fiddler crabs, although smaller crabs also scurry about.

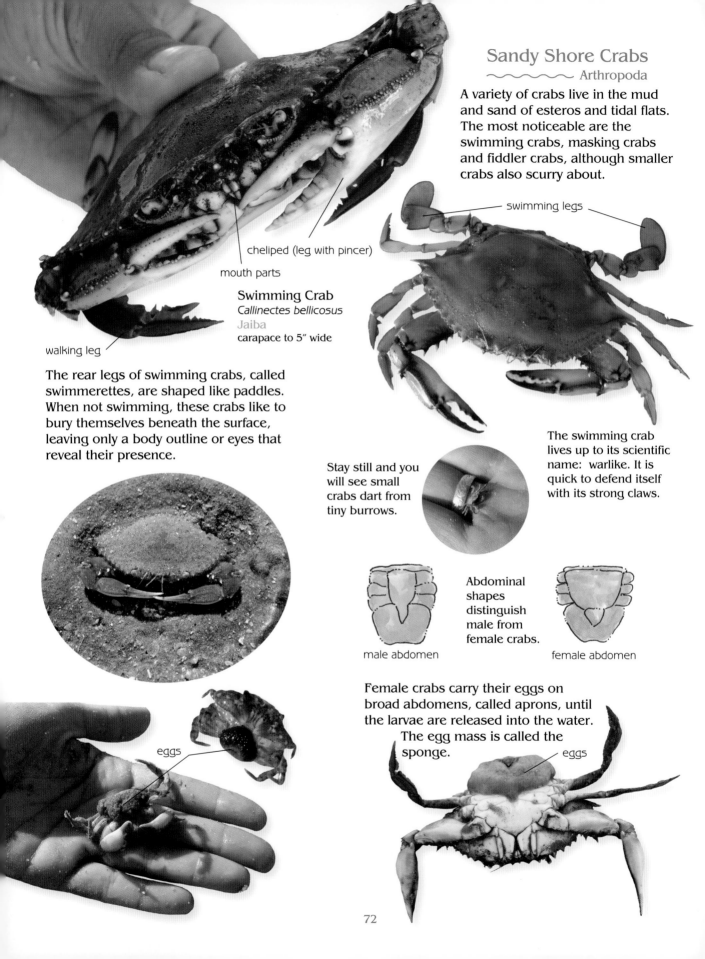

cheliped (leg with pincer)

mouth parts

walking leg

swimming legs

Swimming Crab
Callinectes bellicosus
Jaiba
carapace to 5" wide

The rear legs of swimming crabs, called swimmerettes, are shaped like paddles. When not swimming, these crabs like to bury themselves beneath the surface, leaving only a body outline or eyes that reveal their presence.

Stay still and you will see small crabs dart from tiny burrows.

The swimming crab lives up to its scientific name: warlike. It is quick to defend itself with its strong claws.

Abdominal shapes distinguish male from female crabs.

male abdomen

female abdomen

eggs

Female crabs carry their eggs on broad abdomens, called aprons, until the larvae are released into the water. The egg mass is called the sponge.

eggs

Masking Sand Crabs ～～～～ Arthropoda

A masking or decorator crab's carapace and rough-textured legs are covered with setae (stiff hairs), lumpy bumps and hooked spines. These hooks make it easier for the crab to attach bits of disguise to various areas of its body.

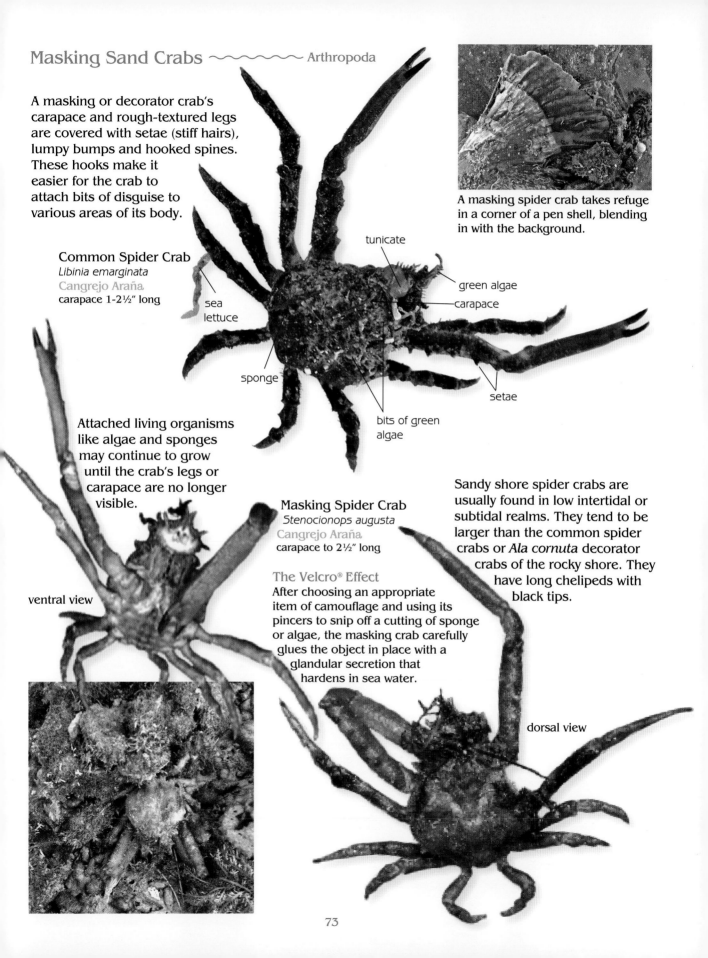

A masking spider crab takes refuge in a corner of a pen shell, blending in with the background.

Common Spider Crab
Libinia emarginata
Cangrejo Araña
carapace 1-2½" long

sea lettuce

tunicate

green algae

carapace

sponge

setae

bits of green algae

Attached living organisms like algae and sponges may continue to grow until the crab's legs or carapace are no longer visible.

ventral view

Masking Spider Crab
Stenocionops augusta
Cangrejo Araña
carapace to 2½" long

The Velcro® Effect
After choosing an appropriate item of camouflage and using its pincers to snip off a cutting of sponge or algae, the masking crab carefully glues the object in place with a glandular secretion that hardens in sea water.

Sandy shore spider crabs are usually found in low intertidal or subtidal realms. They tend to be larger than the common spider crabs or *Ala cornuta* decorator crabs of the rocky shore. They have long chelipeds with black tips.

dorsal view

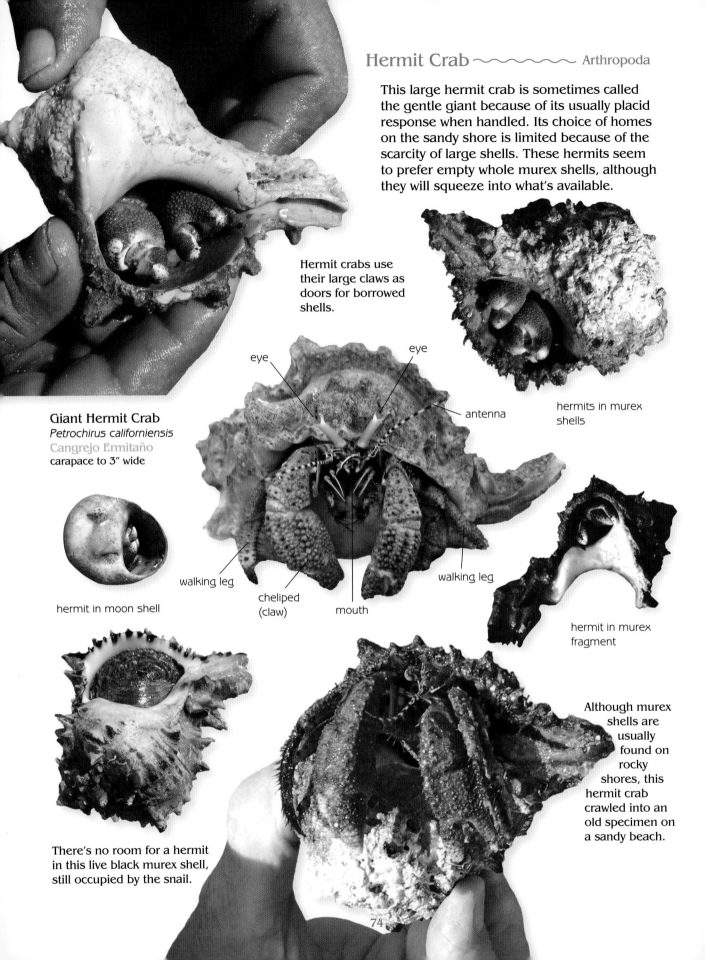

Hermit Crab ⁓⁓⁓⁓⁓⁓ Arthropoda

This large hermit crab is sometimes called the gentle giant because of its usually placid response when handled. Its choice of homes on the sandy shore is limited because of the scarcity of large shells. These hermits seem to prefer empty whole murex shells, although they will squeeze into what's available.

Hermit crabs use their large claws as doors for borrowed shells.

hermits in murex shells

eye eye

antenna

Giant Hermit Crab
Petrochirus californiensis
Cangrejo Ermitaño
carapace to 3" wide

walking leg

walking leg

hermit in moon shell

cheliped (claw)

mouth

hermit in murex fragment

There's no room for a hermit in this live black murex shell, still occupied by the snail.

Although murex shells are usually found on rocky shores, this hermit crab crawled into an old specimen on a sandy beach.

Specialization of Crab Legs and Crab Claws
Scurry, scuttle, sidle, snip, snap, swim

Crabs adapt to their environments in myriad ways. The exoskeletal shapes and musculature of these molluscs vary in response to the demands of survival, locomotion, reproduction and feeding.

Porcelain Crab grasping claw

Porcelain Crab feeding claws

Blue Swimming Crab feeding & fighting claw

Red Reef Crab feeding claw

Blue Swimming Crab feeding & fighting claw

Spider Crab crushing & feeding claw

Cryptic Spider Crab crushing & feeding claw

Masking Crab snipping & decorating chelipeds

Fiddler crab intimidating claw

Blue Swimming Crab swimmerette

Hairy Reef Crab tearing and feeding claw

Giant Hermit Crab defensive & feeding claws

Blue-spotted Hermit Crab locomotory & fighting claws

feeding claw

Lumpy Claw Crab reproductive shielding position

grinding and feeding claw

grasping claw

Lumpy Claw Crab tearing and feeding claw

Crab test feeding claw

Calico Crab snapping claw

Black Reef Crab crushing claw

Fiddler crab intimidating claw

Blue Swimming Crab swimmerettes

walking legs

feeding & fighting claws

Crabs periodically outgrow and discard their shells in a process called molting. The old shell splits across the back and as the split widens, the crab slowly backs out—legs, claws, feelers, mouth parts and all. The soft crab must hide from predators while its new shell hardens and the crab regains its strength. Tidewalkers may find the empty shell (test), or parts of it, on the shore.

molted crab test

Left-handed or right-handed fiddler crabs?
A male fiddler may lose its large right claw in a fight with another male. To speed regeneration, the small left claw grows to become the dominant, intimidating claw while the right one assumes the functions of the secondary, feeding claw. Females and immature males have smaller claws on both sides.

feeding claws

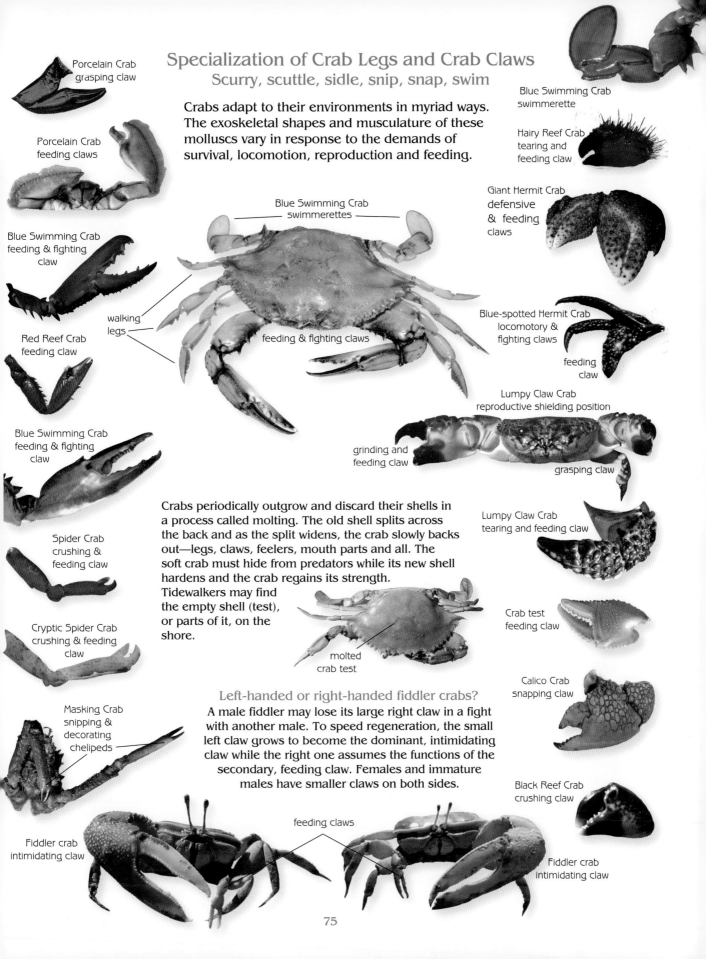

Gulf Sand Star 〜〜 Echinodermata

Gulf Sand Star
Spotted Sand Star
Luidia phragma
Estrella del Mar
to 8" diameter

The colorful gulf sand star, also known as the spotted or beaded sand star, is a sandy shore species. This star was carried to a rocky shore in a violent storm and thrown by waves onto a volcano sponge.

Star rays are essential body parts. They are extensions of the moving, breathing and eating systems.

This gulf sand star begins to right itself, sensing with its tube feet that it is upside down.

Sand star tube feet are pointed at the ends, in contrast to the suction disks at the ends of the tube feet of rocky shore stars. Both types of tube feet are adaptations that allow the star to travel on the substrate of its habitat.

tube feet

This battered star may survive its traumatic tossing onto the reef because it only needs the central disk and one ray to repair its injuries.

Spiny Sand Star ～～～ Echinodermata

Using rows of tube feet the spiny sand star crawls over the surface of sandy and muddy shores where food is most plentiful. It feasts mainly on bivalve molluscs, marine snails and sessile creatures such as barnacles and corals.

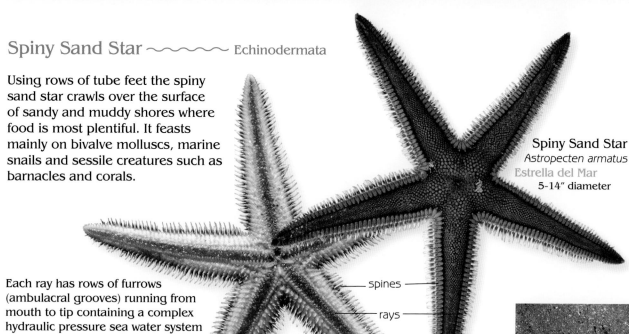

Spiny Sand Star
Astropecten armatus
Estrella del Mar
5-14" diameter

Each ray has rows of furrows (ambulacral grooves) running from mouth to tip containing a complex hydraulic pressure sea water system that operates rows of tube feet. The muscular tube feet in turn control both locomotion and feeding. The star uses strong suction to pry open bivalves; this allows the star to extrude its stomach into the mollusc shell and extract the contents.

spines
rays

The spiny sand star has five flat, beautifully symmetrical rays with beaded margins and a fringe of bristled spines along the sides of each pointed ray.

oral surface

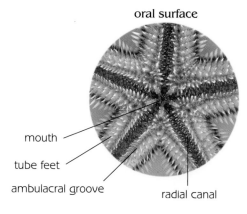

mouth
tube feet
ambulacral groove
radial canal

aboral surface

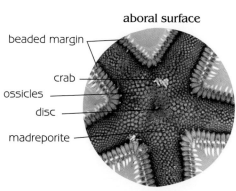

beaded margin
crab
ossicles
disc
madreporite

The exoskeleton of a spiny sea star consists of ossicles (calcareous plates) that fit closely together, rather like a suit of mail, providing both stiffness and flexibility.

The spiny sand star is adept at burrowing quickly under the surface to avoid its enemies and to search for food.

Sand Dollars 〰〰〰 Echinodermata

Sand dollars are related to sea urchins and sea stars. They burrow into the sand, usually below the low tide mark, and filter food while on their edges, positioning so that the feeding side faces the current.

mouth entrance

oral surface

keyhole

Sand dollar skeletons, or tests, are what tidewalkers usually find. The star or petal design shows the five-part radial symmetry characteristic of echinoderms.

ambulacral grooves

The edge has been nibbled, probably by a shark or a ray; however, this sand dollar survived the attack to grow new spines and cilia along the torn edges.

aboral surface

Six-Pored Sand Dollar
Encope micropora
Galleta del Mar
5" diameter

Sand dollars expose themselves to the water current to collect organic particles that drift by.

Sand dollar tests can be difficult to see in the water.

aboral surface

Keyhole Sand Dollar skeleton
Encope grandis
Galleta del Mar
4" diameter

lunule or slot

cilia

Cilia (hairs) encase tiny spines used to gather and move food into the mouth at the center of the oral surface.

pore

oral surface

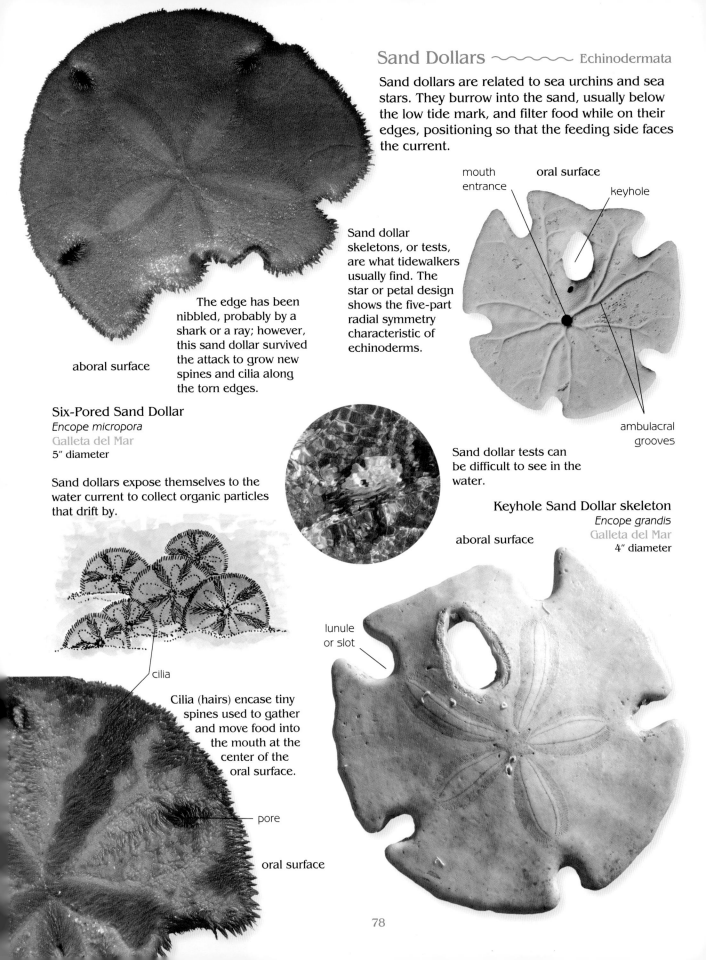

Tidewalking: Muddy Flats and Esteros

Gulf esteros are negative estuaries—they no longer receive a reliable flow of fresh water. As a result, tides perform the function of flushing and cleaning the water in an estero. Mud flats and esteros in the Sea of Cortez are affected by tidal fluctuations twice daily, just as on rocky or sandy shores.

clay clumps

Without a source of fresh water, salinity in an estero rises. Moisture evaporates under the hot sun, placing sand and soil at the mercy of the wind. Clay clumps form, changing the composition and texture of the animal habitats.

Estero at high tide

Estero at low tide

This place, seemingly barren, actually teems with subtle life. Marine muds contain vital nutrients for animals that burrow beneath the surface.

Ancient silts, deposited when rivers flowed into the sea, form fine clay sediments, resulting in a perfect environment for wild and cultivated oysters.

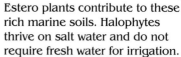

The muddy shore is used by molluscs, shrimp, crabs, fish and birds as a nursery for their young.

wild oysters

cultivated oysters

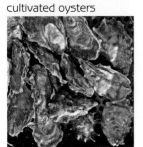

Estero plants contribute to these rich marine soils. Halophytes thrive on salt water and do not require fresh water for irrigation.

Oyster farms are a familiar sight in the estuaries and esteros of modern Mexico. The primary species that is farmed is not native to the Gulf.

Slogging through mud requires determined tidewalking, but it is well worth the effort to see the wide variety of creatures living on a muddy shore.

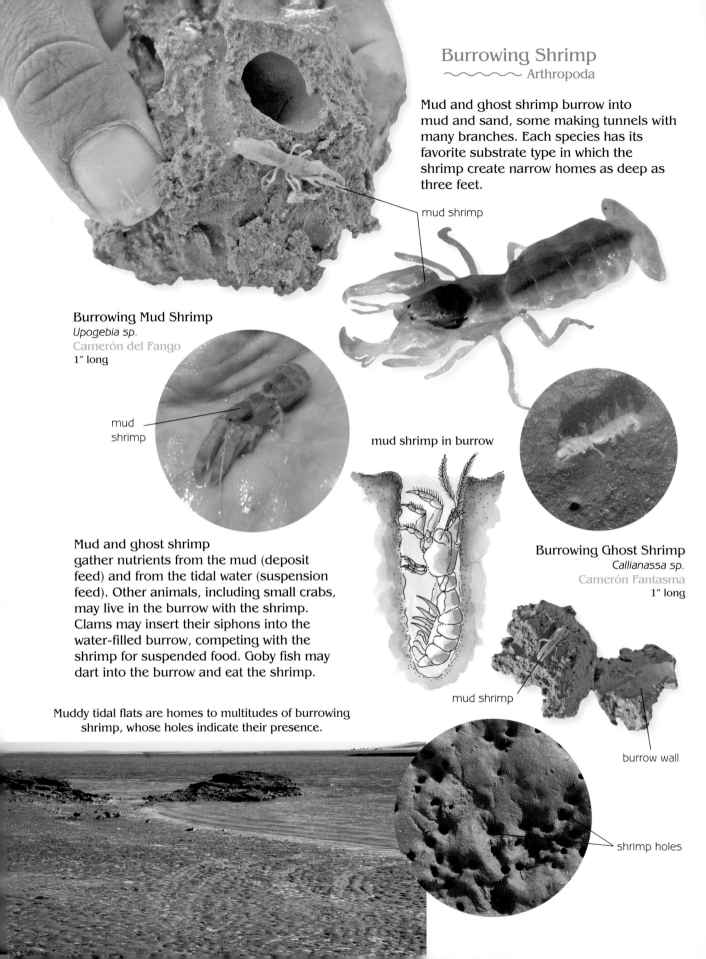

Burrowing Shrimp
~~~~~~~~ Arthropoda

Mud and ghost shrimp burrow into mud and sand, some making tunnels with many branches. Each species has its favorite substrate type in which the shrimp create narrow homes as deep as three feet.

mud shrimp

Burrowing Mud Shrimp
Upogebia sp.
Camerón del Fango
1" long

mud shrimp

mud shrimp in burrow

Mud and ghost shrimp gather nutrients from the mud (deposit feed) and from the tidal water (suspension feed). Other animals, including small crabs, may live in the burrow with the shrimp. Clams may insert their siphons into the water-filled burrow, competing with the shrimp for suspended food. Goby fish may dart into the burrow and eat the shrimp.

Burrowing Ghost Shrimp
Callianassa sp.
Camerón Fantasma
1" long

mud shrimp

burrow wall

Muddy tidal flats are homes to multitudes of burrowing shrimp, whose holes indicate their presence.

shrimp holes

Fiddler Crabs ～～～ Arthropoda

Fiddler crabs are poor swimmers and prefer to burrow in mud and sand just below the high tide line. Fiddler crab males wave their large front claw to attract females, warn intruders and claim territory.

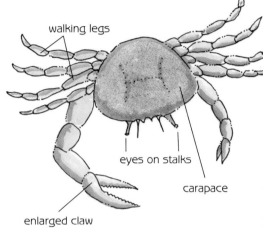

walking legs

eyes on stalks

carapace

enlarged claw

Fiddler crabs have pigment-bearing cells that cause them to change colors in response to the tides and the time of day. Fiddler activities are governed by a tidal biorhythm, an inborn sense of where the water is.

Uca musica

At low tide thousands of fiddler crabs come out of their burrows to eat and court, rushing back home to safety if they detect a threat. Although they cannot see well, fiddlers' compound eyes give them a 360 degree visual field. Fiddlers can also sense vibrations in the sand.

mastication balls

Fiddlers feed by scraping mud with their claws, then using the mouth parts to select bits of organic material to eat. After dinner they roll the leftover mud into small mastication balls and put them outside the burrow.

burrow

Uca crenulata

Princely Fiddler Crab
Uca princeps
Cangrejo Violinista
carapace to 2" wide

Female fiddlers may check fifty male burrows before deciding on a mate!

Three fiddler species:
•*Uca musica* (purple) is the smallest fiddler and likes the highest zone farthest away from the water.
•*Uca crenulata* (red) is middle-sized and prefers the mid-tide area.
•*Uca princeps* (blue) is the largest and likes to be in the lower, wetter zone.

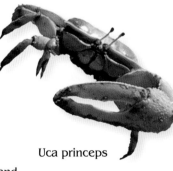

Uca princeps

Pacific Worm Eel
Chordata

Pacific Worm Eel
Myrophis vafer
Tiezo Lombriz
to 10" long

Longtail Goby
Gobionellis sagittula
Góbio
to 4½" long

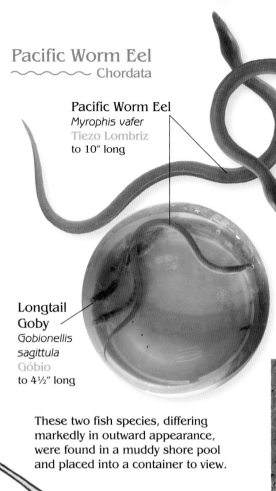

This worm-like estero dweller is a fish, usually seen writhing in shallow water. Attempts to catch the Pacific worm eel will often fail as it will slither speedily back under the surface when touched. This eel is harmless, although it does have small teeth.

These two fish species, differing markedly in outward appearance, were found in a muddy shore pool and placed into a container to view.

The Pacific worm eel's family name, Ophichthidae, is derived from two Greek words, ophis—serpent and ichthys—fish.

Round Sting Ray
Urolophus halleri
Mantaraya
body 1-2' diameter

Sting Ray
Chordata

poisonous spine

pectoral wing

sting ray depression in sand

eye

The infamous sting ray resides in the northern Gulf and, especially during the warmer months, comes close to shore to mate and hunt. The ray swims by waving its pectoral wings above the sand, gulping crabs, small fish and molluscs as it cruises. When the ray burrows, only its eyes may show above the surface. Sensing vibrations, it is ready to sting with its poisonous tail spine if stepped upon.

To avoid a painful and potentially dangerous sting, watch where you place your feet when walking in the sea. A good technique is to do the sting ray shuffle: slide your feet, rather than step down in order to scare the rays away. If you are stung with the poisonous spine, submerging the injury in hot water is recommended to draw the venom out. Get medical treatment as soon as possible to minimize the chance of infection.

Halophytes ～～～ Anthrophyta

Esteros and tidal flats are harsh habitats, challenging all but a few plants. Those that do thrive are called halophytes, or salt plants. They are able to grow in water that is more saline than most plants can tolerate.

Pickleweed
Salicornia sp.

Salicornia's popular name is pickleweed. Its segments resemble pickles. Salicornia tastes tangy and salty and is a candidate for experimental agriculture on desert coastlines.

Salt Grass, Wild Wheat
Distichlis palmeri
Arroz del Mar

Sometimes mistaken for Bermuda grass, this endemic grain-bearing salt grass has been harvested by Gulf area indigenous people.

Iodine Bush
Allenrolfea occidentalis
Chamizo

Halophytes use special strategies to survive in the tidal flats and esteros. Many are succulents, storing water in their tissues, while others excrete excess salt. Flexible and ground-hugging halophyte shapes resist damage from moving water.

This low-lying grass grows in prickly masses in intertidal mud.

Shore Grass
Monanthochloe littoralis
Zacate playero

Estuary Sea-Blite
Suaeda esteroa

Work and Play

Observing seashore lifeways adds to one's understanding of those who live by the sea. The shore invokes wonder, brings joy, excites curiosity, inspires scientific research, raises conservation passions, provides work, encourages arts and crafts and suggests tasty seafood dishes. Many seacoast efforts and enterprises are unique to the shore. The edge of the sea is a special place.

FISH MARKET

OYSTERS

Fishing takes many forms.

snorkeling 101

tidepool contortionist

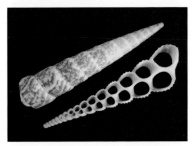

tower shell and cross section

clamdiggers

Shallow water sailing is great sport for children of all ages.

Palapa construction is a time-honored craft in most tropical seaside cultures around the world.

Beach vendors peddle hats, sunglasses, jewelry, and local arts and crafts.

Dune rolling can be irresistible fun!

Boat launchers always have work in beach and fishing communities.

Seri Indian ironwood carvings

Tools

pack

hat

Although the essential tool on a tidepool trip is curiosity, the items on this page may increase your pleasure and enhance your comfort and safety.

camera

Record your discoveries—a digital camera is a good choice, as is a pen and pad.

water

Always carry water!

vest

sun block

Gloves are useful, but not essential.

gloves

pen & pad

MEMO

insect repellant

A loupe or magnifying glass will reveal fascinating details.

towel

Have a towel handy (pin it to your clothes).

magnifying glass

loupe

Reef shoes help your feet grip the boulders and protect against cuts and scrapes.

pail

shoes

plastic dish

net

trowel

computer mouse pads stapled together make good knee pads

The tidewalkers' lab: a pail and dish make a portable and inexpensive way to examine tidepool algae and animals before you return them to the sea.

We hope that you find the treasures of the sea as beautiful and as fascinating as we do. We also hope that you enjoy them in their natural environment, disturb them as little as possible, and leave even empty shells where you find them. You never know when a hermit crab will be looking for a new home. Please turn the rocks back over!

Flotsam and Jetsam

Beach debris includes evidence of intertidal and deep water life, human activity and carelessness. The sea cleans the beach at one tide and deposits its gatherings at the next. Things that float are called flotsam and things thrown (jettisoned) into the sea are called jetsam. A little-used term is lagan: things that have been tied to a buoy for later retrieval.

Can you find this trowel elsewhere in the book?

Findings in this strandline drift include a piece of rope, fish bones, dried algae, string, shells and feathers. Nearby is the shoeprint of a curious tidewalker.

after the party

Life-style leftovers, benign curiosities or debris dangerous to man and intertidal creatures—flotsam and jetsam add interest to a tidewalk. It's OK to bring a trash bag to the beach!

someone lost a serape

one of many

swimsam?

earring

tennis anyone?

broken glass—ouch!

spark plug

mermaid school?

Key to inside front cover puzzle

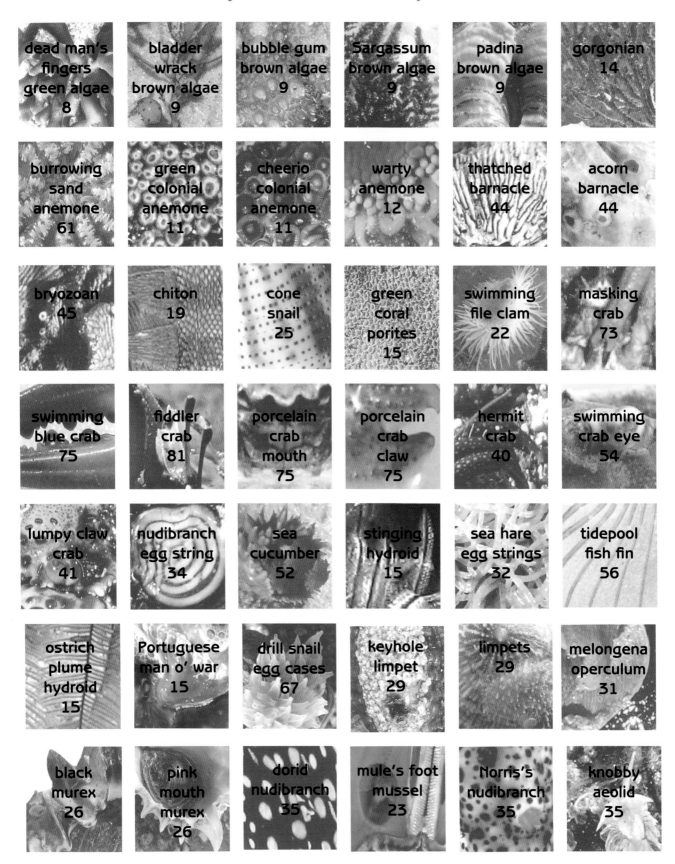

dead man's fingers green algae 8

bladder wrack brown algae 9

bubble gum brown algae 9

Sargassum brown algae 9

padina brown algae 9

gorgonian 14

burrowing sand anemone 61

green colonial anemone 11

cheerio colonial anemone 11

warty anemone 12

thatched barnacle 44

acorn barnacle 44

bryozoan 45

chiton 19

cone snail 25

green coral porites 15

swimming file clam 22

masking crab 73

swimming blue crab 75

fiddler crab 81

porcelain crab mouth 75

porcelain crab claw 75

hermit crab 40

swimming crab eye 54

lumpy claw crab 41

nudibranch egg string 34

sea cucumber 52

stinging hydroid 15

sea hare egg strings 32

tidepool fish fin 56

ostrich plume hydroid 15

Portuguese man o' war 15

drill snail egg cases 67

keyhole limpet 29

limpets 29

melongena operculum 31

black murex 26

pink mouth murex 26

dorid nudibranch 35

mule's foot mussel 23

Norris's nudibranch 35

knobby aeolid 35

nudibranch sedna 34	two-spotted octopus 37	pygmy octopus 71	turban operculum 31	pelican foot 57	colonial anemone 11
pen shell 66	egg strings 66	pen shell 4	calico scallop 62	limpet 29	sand dollar 78
scallop 62	ghost shrimp 80	pistol shrimp 38	sea hare 32	tunicate 53	rock snail 26
spiny sand star 77	spiny sand star 77	bristle star 46	brittle star 47	Panamic brittle star 46	spiny sand star 77
heliaster sun star 48	heliaster sun star mouth 48	sun star sucker feet 48	Gulf sand star 60	Gulf sand star 76	Gulf sand star 76
trivia coffee bean 27	slate pencil urchin 51	spiny urchin 50	ripples 55	feather duster tube worm 18	fire worm 17
flatworm 16	lug worm extrusion 60	amphitrite medusa worm 17	segmented sand worm 17	burrowing sand anemone 61	flatworm 16

The Upper Gulf of California

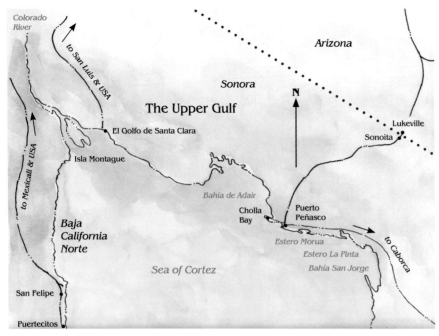

The upper Gulf has been influenced by eons of Colorado River flow. Though the flow is now a trickle compared to past centuries, the river's deposited sediment makes the upper Gulf shallow, without the deep basins of the midriff and southern regions. Both land and sea experience summer and winter, reflected in the seasonal variety of marine invertebrates and algae.

rocky

muddy

sandy

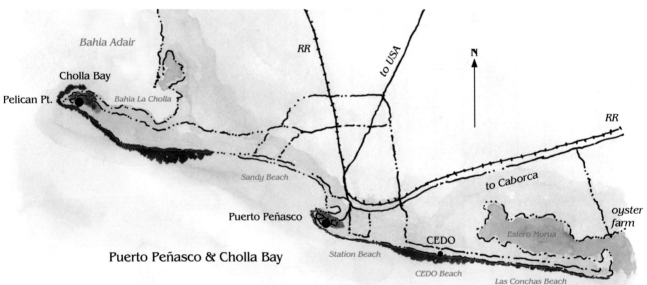

Puerto Peñasco & Cholla Bay

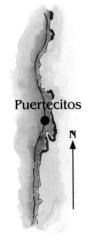

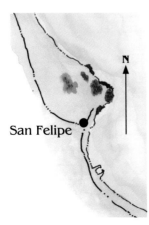

These sketch maps, though not to scale, show the approximate locations of the most easily reached shorelines in the northern Gulf and the general character of the beaches. For detailed directions consult highway maps. Talk to travel agents, dive shop personnel, fishing club members and community residents about current access. Visit CEDO (Puerto Peñasco) for species updates and conservation concerns. Bookstores and the internet are rich resources where you can gather more information before your trip.

To Learn More

Beckvar, Nancy, Richard Norris and Sherman Suter. Reprinted from Flessa, K. W. (ed) 1987. Keys to the Shells of Bahia La Choya, Sonora, Mexico. University of Arizona. Tucson, AZ

Brusca, Richard C. 1980. Common Intertidal Invertebrates of the Gulf of California, 2nd edition. The University of Arizona Press. Tucson, AZ

Brusca, Richard C., Erin Kimrey and Wendy Moore (eds). 2004. A Seashore Guide to the Northern Gulf of California. Arizona-Sonora Desert Museum. Tucson, AZ   .

Farmer, Wesley M. 1968. Tidepool Animals from the Gulf of California. Wesword Company. San Diego, CA

Gotshall, Daniel W. 1998. Sea of Cortez Marine Animals. Sea Challengers. Monterey, CA

Houston, Roy S. 2006. Natural History Guide to the Northwestern Gulf of California and Adjacent Desert. Xlibris, USA

Keen, Myra. 1971. Sea Shells of Tropical West America. Stanford University Press. Stanford, CA

Kerstitch, Alex and Hans Bertsch. 2007. Sea of Cortez Marine Invertebrates, 2nd edition (Revised). Sea Challengers, Monterey, CA

McKibbin, Nonie. 1989. The Sea in the Desert. Golden Puffer Press. Tucson, AZ

Readdie, Mark D., Marla Ranelletti and Richard M. McCourt. Common Seaweeds of the Gulf of California. Sea Challengers. Monterey, CA

Steinbeck, John. 1951. The Log from the Sea of Cortez. Viking Press. New York, NY

Thomson, Donald A. and Nonie McKibbin. 1976. Gulf of California Fishwatcher's Guide. Golden Puffer Press. Tucson, AZ

Thomson, Donald A., Lloyd T. Findley and Alex N. Kerstitch. 1979. Reef Fishes of the Sea of Cortez. John Wiley & Sons, New York

Violette, Paul E. 1964. Shelling in the Sea of Cortez. Dale Stuart King. Tucson, AZ

Warr, Diana and Albert Collier. 1982. Seashore Biology Notes: A Field Guide to the Common Animals in the Northern Gulf of California Tidepools, 2nd edition. Winter Publishing Company. Tucson, AZ

Index

Index

Key to identification:
Common Name
Latin name
Spanish Name
size

    Red=safety notes

The Authors and
The Edge of the Sea of Cortez

Marilyn Malone and Betty Hupp

We became close friends in the early 1980's working in the University of Arizona Graphics Department. Our eight young children often played together on the beach at Marilyn's home in Puerto Peñasco, Mexico. What we needed then, but couldn't find, was a guidebook to consult for answers to our children's questions about the critters in the tide pools. As avid beach-combers, we invariably concluded that we should write such a book ourselves, but as the busy mothers-of-many, we simply never found the time. Fortunately our beach book dream was still alive when digital cameras took the world by storm.

After retirement from our respective careers (Marilyn as a police officer and detective in Tucson and Betty as an executive assistant at the Universities of Arizona and Vermont), our bright idea became an obsession. Four years of research were sandwiched between frequent photographic trips to the Sea of Cortez. With encouragement from university faculty researchers and local science teachers and CEDO. we designed and organized the book mainly as a guide for marine biology students of all ages on field trips to Mexico. We wanted to make the topics equally understandable for families visiting beach resort communities. Currently, we are planning future tidewalking adventures on Pacific, Mediterranean or Caribbean shores with our young grandchildren.

Acknowledgments and I

University of Arizona friends

Dr. Katrina Mangin, Dr.   rdians of scientific accuracy
Heather Green and Alys   g companions
Peter Kresan—photography and technical advisor
Katherine Larson—
Norman Meader—
Dr. Joseph Schreib
Dr. Arthur Vokes, A

CEDO friends

Peggy Turk Boyer,   or
Rick Boyer, CEDO /   dvisor
Sofia Lopez Alvirde   and beach critter afficionados
The CEDO staff and   nd pleasant

Tucson friends

Dr. Richard Brusca,   d trip guru
Carrie Dean, Audub
James Gregg, Arizo   nposition critic
Katie Iverson, Pima   ultant
Jenean Thomson—
Gail Ballweber, Ariz
Marilyn Kessler, Ariz   gn® collaborator

Puerto Peñasco friends

Albert and Sue Kind
Sally Dalton, Xochitl'
Guy and Linda Scho   sts

Without the technical assi   se amazing and inspirational
individuals, our book wou   ave been possible without the
patience and forebearanc   ing in our book!

                                                           and Marilyn Malone